I Once Was a Nice Guy:

The hilarious and psychotic tales about the women of my past

Based on true stories

By: Juddy Ferguson

© 2014, Juddy Ferguson Self publishing

www.juddyferguson.com

ALL RIGHTS RESERVED. This book contains material protected under International and Federal Copyright Laws and Treaties. Any unauthorized reprint or use of this material is prohibited. No part of this book may be reproduced or transmitted in any form or by any means, electronic or mechanical, including photocopying, recording, or by any information storage and retrieval system without express written permission from the author / publisher

Acknowledgements:

I want to formally thank the wonderful people who have helped me bring this book to life. The support and guidance you have given me will never be forgotten. Love you with all my heart:

My Family

Calvin

Nathan

Sarah

Steven & Rebecca

John & Megan

Kristi

Dedication:

This book is dedicated to anyone who has had their heart ripped to shreds.

Table of Contents:

Intro

The Beginning of the End

Chapter 1-Jayden: 'The Alcoholic Brainiac' Part 1

Chapter 2-Jayden: 'The Alcoholic Brainiac' Part 2

Chapter 3-Jayden: 'The Alcoholic Brainiac' Part 3

Chapter 4-Ravenna: 'The Cocaine Tree Giant' Part 1

Chapter 5-Ravenna: 'The Cocaine Tree Giant' Part 2

Chapter 6-Sydnie: 'The Freshman Snake'

Chapter 7-Gretchen: 'The Psychotic Gremlin' Part 1

Chapter 8-Gretchen: 'The Psychotic Gremlin' Part 2

Chapter 9-Gretchen: 'The Psychotic Gremlin' Part 3

Chapter 10-Carlisle: 'The Virtual Girlfriend'

Chapter 11-Aberdeen: 'The Double Crossing Ice Dancer'

Chapter 12-Chandler: 'The Personal Trainer Sex Fiend'

Chapter 13-Fawn: 'The Wasted Witch'

Chapter 14-Love Is Dangerous

Revenge Is Near

The Awakening

Intro

Hello there, friends, my name is Juddy; not to be confused with Judy, but simply, Buddy with a J. In my life I have had that unfortunate pleasure of dating some of the most psychotic, manipulative, and deceitful women that have ever existed on this earth. I now believe that a few of them may not even be human. These accusations may seem a bit drastic, but as you dive head first into these tales of tragedy, you will find that the descriptions are entirely accurate.

Before I decide to expose you to my many misfortunes with the opposite sex, I would like to tell you a little bit about myself.

Treating a woman right was one of the things I always believed I was good at. I did everything in my power to be loving, polite, and kind. I was not born with these specific qualities. I owe that to the two people that know me the best, my parents.

I grew up in a very loving home. Watching their relationship as a child over the years made me realize how happy they really were. They had some arguments from time to time, but who doesn't? They would normally end with my father telling my mother, "I'm sorry," or "It's not mine, I was just holding it for a friend."

My parents wanted to make sure that I would one day be molded into a gentleman along with my two younger brothers. They began teaching me the proper etiquette basics as I grew up. Then one day, at the age of thirteen, both of my testicles descended, and my voice became much deeper. I immediately alerted my father, and he calmly said, "It is time my son."

My parents enrolled me into a Junior Cotillion. It was a three-day event that included lessons about table manners, proper etiquette, and ballroom dancing. The cotillion had over a hundred participants mixed with guys and girls. Most of the guys were there as punishment, and most of the girls were there for the ballroom dancing.

The dancing lesson was definitely the lamest part of the entire event. Unfortunately, our partners were chosen at random, so we didn't have a choice. I was one of the shortest guys there so ironically I was paired with the tallest girl at the entire Cotillion. She had a good six inches on me. It was like dancing with a tree trunk.

My female dancing partner apparently was going for a 'Greek Goddess' type of look. She had what looked to be poison ivy, or some sort of green vine wrapped around her hair and dress. This 'greenery' was my perfect escape plan.

I explained, "I'm sorry. I have a plant allergy. I'm unfit to be your dance partner."

She said in an angry voice, "It's fake you idiot!"

"I'm sorry. I can't take the risk."

The cotillion was a good foundation to set me on the right path to being a well-mannered young man. However, the most I ever learned was from my father. He always told me that he knew everything there was to know about women, which in my opinion was scientifically impossible. I later came to find out that most of my father's teachings originated from George Washington's book titled *Rules of Civility & Decent Behavior In Company and Conversation.* I was required to read it front to back. The novel included lessons on proper table manners, respecting others, and presenting one's self as a true gentleman.

With the combination of my parent's teachings, the cotillion, and the book, I made sure I followed these rules no matter what. In doing so, I was hoping that one day I would find the love of my life.

Relationship articles are always flooding the Web like a virus these days. The majority of them typically point the finger at the man as being the villain. Titles such as, *'Ten signs your husband is cheating on you',* or *'Seven reasons why you should dump your boyfriend'* are always popping up on my search engine.

As a guy, I know that men can be ruthless douchebags, however in my experience girls can be just as bad. I believe that guys and girls are equally malicious. It's not that one gender is worse than the other. No matter what, there will always be evil creatures hiding in the shadows on both sides.

Everyone on this planet that is looking for love deserves someone that will treat them right and make them happy. Unfortunately, finding that special person can sometimes be a brutal and daunting task.

In chronological order, I would like you take a journey with me into the dark and desolate world of my ex-girlfriends. It's a place filled with fear, anger, and extremely awkward sexual escapades.

These are the tales of where in another life, I once, was a nice guy…

The Beginning of the End

I slowly walked through the front door of a run-down bar. It had been raining all day, and my clothes were soaked. Cigarette smoke filled the place like a morning fog. I took a seat near the back and ordered a drink. I had not been here in awhile, but things hadn't changed much.

I could see cobwebs on the ceiling, and I could hear the faint cries of a busted jukebox. There was a pool table next to me covered in dust, and the air was decrepit.

Once my drink arrived I stared into the Mason jar in front of me that was filled with my favorite poison. With every sip, the sharp burn of old whiskey traveled down my throat. It seemed that my drinking had become worse over the years.

Depression had been haunting me for a very long time, and I found myself unable to control it anymore. I had been swimming in a sea of madness for far too long. My mind had lost its way, and my reality had become a desolate world filled with pain and anger.

I had become a recluse, hiding from the world. I had stopped taking care of myself, and I hadn't shaved in months. My beard and mustache had grown quite a bit. My facial hair was long, scraggly, and coarse.

I was also forty pounds overweight due to the heavy drinking and lack of exercise.

This wasn't like me. This was never like me.

As I began to drown my feelings in alcohol, the emotional trauma became more intense. Never in my life have I been so uncertain about the future.

Love didn't exist anymore. It had been slowly destroyed by the women of my past. Why did they do these horrible things to me? What have I done to deserve this? I never wanted it to end this way. I never wanted to hurt anyone.

For too long I had made grave mistakes in the search for happiness. The fear of loneliness had grown inside me like a disease.

I didn't feel like talking to anyone, but I wasn't alone that night. There was someone at the table with me. Someone I had met before.

"Do you know how badly I want to kill you?" I said.

"Yes…I do."

I need to go back to the very beginning, where it all started. Only there would I find the reasons for my madness...

Chapter 1-Jayden: 'The Alcoholic Brainiac' Part 1

I had my backpack strapped tight, my shirt tucked in, and my hair greased up with an enormous amount of styling glue. I was a bit nervous as I entered the large dining hall. I was getting peculiar looks from most of the students, but I didn't blame them. I was the new guy in town, and I looked like a geek.

It was the first day of my sophomore year in a new high school. The smell of puberty and sack lunches was in the air. There was a strict dress code, and anti-PDA posters scattered all over the eggshell white walls. There was Chapel twice a week, and one hour of outdoor time each day. The outside of the school had a barbed wire fence surrounding the private Christian fortress. It was more like a prison than anything else.

During the first few weeks of school, I was an outsider. No one could get my name right; Judy, Jody, Judith, they didn't know what to call me. I was just a floater trying to find a social group.

Steven was the first friend I made at school. He was the class clown of our sophomore class. He played football and was a pretty husky fellow. He was also a 'regular' in detention.

"Hey, man, I'm Steven. I'm the guy who will be cheating off your paper.

He then chuckled heavily like a barbarian.

"In return, I will introduce you to the lamest high school in history," he said.

"Thanks, I feel like an outcast," I replied with a sigh of relief.

I was sixteen, and girls were all over my radar screen. It was about one girl to every five guys, and the selection of attractive women was very limited. The best-looking girls were already spoken for, including one in particular who had caught my eye right off the bat. Her name was Jayden.

The guys at school referred to her as the bodacious blonde. She had long straight hair, and some of the whitest teeth I'd ever seen. It was like she gargled a cup of bleach every morning.

She was about five-foot-seven and one of the only girls to quickly blossom with ripe coconuts. Her skin was lightly tanned with just a few freckles on her cheeks. She had a slim athletic build and some nice legs.

Jayden was a pre-packaged Barbie doll…with a brain.

She was extremely intelligent. Jayden was academically ranked number two in the entire sophomore class, and was also enrolled in every honors class that existed. She never got in trouble, always made straight A's, and had a crystal clean slate. She was almost untouchable.

Unfortunately for me, Jayden was currently dating a guy named George. He was a popular football player who was a bit of a dimwit. Regardless, he was the only lad worthy enough to date the sophomore queen at the time.

My father always taught me to never get in the middle of something special between two people. He would say, "If she is meant to be with you, then an opportunity will present itself. Don't ever force it."

I stood back and just began to observe the couple at school. It was creepy, and I felt like the guy on 'American Beauty' with the camcorder.

They would eat lunch together, hold hands every chance they got, and often rode to school in the same car. They looked happy and it was almost picture perfect.

As I was building friendships with the students in our sophomore class, I was getting invited to parties more often. Among the partygoers that were 'shot-gunning' beers and funneling liquor, I would often see Jayden and George together.

Jayden was a social butterfly, and George was a pothead.

A match made in heaven.

They would always end up fighting about something, and end up leaving the party early. The fights began to transpire at school as well. Often times, they would be arguing in the hallways against the lockers. Something told me these confrontations had to do with marijuana.

I always kept my distance from the two of them and never interfered. I would have gotten my ass kicked by the entire football team if I ever spoke to her. Suddenly, Jayden and I began to exchange looks at school while passing each other in the hallways. She would smile and say, "Hey, Juddy!"

She knew I existed, and that was one small step towards the acquisition of her company.

A few weeks later, the infamous couple had a huge fight after school in the parking lot. There was yelling and screaming on both sides. They inevitably broke up, and George peeled out of the parking lot like one tough badass. Jayden was finally unshackled, and was no longer a prisoner.

The next day at school was pure pandemonium. The cafeteria had turned into the New York stock exchange. All the guys were running around with their heads cut off, trying to form a plan to capture the recently released, Jayden Matthews. I had to be careful of how I calculated my attack because obviously, I wasn't the only man who had her in their crosshairs.

All of the teenage bloodhounds were ready to go above the call of duty to win her affection. The competition was stiff because I was up against older dudes who had cars and money. I rode to school with my mom and was broke as shit.

Every single guy that went after her crashed and burned. I could see the lack of enthusiasm on Jayden's face each time she was aggressively approached. She wasn't impressed whatsoever by these acts of valor.

How was I going to capture the heart of Jayden?

Steven was throwing a party on Friday night at his house. Word traveled fast up and down the school halls. Everyone that was 'cool' was going. I had to ask Jayden a futile question. I passed her in the hallway multiple times that day, but I never had the courage to make a move. The fear of a rejection was creeping over my shoulders, and I was utterly afraid to approach her.

Finally, at the end of the day, I saw her in the cafeteria standing alone.

Time to grow a pair of nuts.

I ran up to her and said, "Hey are you going to Steven's party?"

"Hey, Juddy! Yeah I'll probably go. I literally live two blocks away," she said.

"Oh great! See you there!"

It felt like I had just unwrapped my first gift on Christmas Day!

That following Friday, we got everything set up at Steven's house, and the party was on. People began to show up early around 8pm because a lot of us had curfews. As our friends funneled through the front door, we were passing out drinks as fast as we could make them. We packed about a hundred people in that house, and we were close to max capacity. If a fire broke out, we would probably all die, but that was a risk we were willing to take.

Time began to fly by. It was about 11pm, and Jayden still hadn't shown up. I had guzzled about ten beers and three shots of the shitty tequila. I was shitfaced and could barely stand up straight.

Suddenly, Steven came running over to me. He had his cell phone in one hand, and a beer in the other.

"Jayden is on the phone for you dude. Don't fuck it up," he said.

I replied, "I'll do my best."

"Hello?"

As if I didn't know who it was.

"Hey it's Jayden. I just wanted to let you know that I can't make it tonight. I'm sorry," she said.

"What if I come on you?"

"What did you just say?"

"Sorry. I mean. What if I come to you?"

"Well, I can maybe meet you outside, but I have to be careful about my parents."

"Don't worry. I have ninja stealth skills. I'm on my way."

"Um, ok. Just be careful."

Boy did I fuck that up.

Jayden gave me directions to her house. They were pretty simple, but again, I was hammered.

The house was only about ten minutes away. I wandered around that damn neighborhood for over an hour. It felt like I was trapped in a suburbia maze without any escape.

Finally, I arrived at the large white house, which had a huge front lawn and tall trees. At the top of the trees were large bright lights that illuminated the entire area. I had to be careful and make sure her parents didn't catch me in the spotlights. As I hid in the bushes like a pedophile, I sent her a text message to let her know I had arrived.

As I was attempting to sneak my way up to the front door by staying in the shadows, Jayden walked out onto the front porch. I could hear her laughing.

"There's no need to avoid the lights Juddy. My parents are dead asleep," she said.

I felt like a dumbass.

She was wearing sweat pants and a hoodie. For some strange reason, that turned me on. We just sat on her porch and talked for a while. My slurred voice was quite embarrassing.

"Would youuu like to-go-to a restaurant with meee?" I asked.

Jayden laughed and said, "Yeah sure. Will we have dinner as well?"

"Whatever you want."

"As long as we get to eat, I would love to go!"

"Dinner it is my princess!

"Princess?"

"Sorry. I'm little drunk."

"A little?"

The alcohol inside me wanted to lean in for a sloppy drunk kiss. I used the small shred of self-control I had to stop my mouth from opening. We hugged each other goodbye, and I began my journey back to the party.

Inevitably, I got lost again. All I saw were empty roads and streetlights. I walked what seemed like a few miles.

When I finally arrived, Steven's house was a disaster. It looked like a beer bomb had exploded and the suds were dripping from the walls. I tried to search for a couch that was not occupied or covered in vomit. The only piece of furniture I could find was a futon chair. I curled up inside of it like a fetus and passed out.

I don't know exactly why Jayden said yes to me that night. Did she feel obligated because I had left the party and made the treacherous journey to see her? Was it my silver braces shining in the moonlight? The world may never know.

And so, the first date of my life was about to begin. I only had one shot at this, and I wanted to do it right.

Luckily, I had recently picked up a part time job at the movie theatre. I was appointed to the usher position due to my lack of experience in the film industry. At least it was a steady paycheck, and it kept my wallet somewhat filled.

I had to go into my secret stash in order to have enough money for the date. I also gathered all the coins I could find around the house, and went to the coin-to-cash machine at the grocery store. I had gathered about $100 dollars and was ready for action.

It took some heavy negotiating to get my parents to let me have the car for the evening. They granted me access as long as I brought it back with a full tank.

The transportation was secure. Now it was on to the outfit.

I went into my closet to search my small array of fabrics. I picked out a nice blue flannel button down shirt and my favorite pair of overpriced Abercrombie jeans. I then covered myself from head to toe in Old Spice body spray. The final step was the most important.

The hair styling and gel application.

I drenched my hair in a mixture of hot water and clear gel. I then used a comb to part my hair evenly down the middle like the Red Sea. Once that was done, I used a can of hair spray to put on a final coat for maximum hold. This would ensure that not even a hurricane would have an effect on my perfectly parted hairstyle.

I was extremely nervous, so I tried to follow the proper procedures in order to guarantee a successful date. First off, I made sure I was on time. Dinner was at 7:30pm, so I left my house promptly at 6:45pm. I arrived at Jayden's house right at 7:00pm. I felt like a robot, with braces.

The fear that ran down my spine when I first pulled into Jayden's driveway was something I will never forget.

Don't screw this up, Juddy. Be cool.

I knocked on the front door and Jayden emerged. She looked beautiful. She was wearing a causal navy blue dress that was wrapped with a white sweater.

"Hello, Jayden. You look very nice," I said.

"So do you! Thanks for picking me up," she replied.

I walked her out to the car, and opened the door for her. We set off into the sunset in my father's silver four-door Volvo.

We had decided on dinner and a movie. We went to a small Mexican restaurant not too from her house. As we walked in, the place was jam-packed. It was a local hotspot with the best fajitas in town. As the waiters were walking past us carrying trays filled with steaming meat and rice, my hunger became overwhelming.

Once we sat down, we blankly stared at each other for an extended amount of time. I didn't know how to break the ice. It was as if I had forgotten the English language. I could feel the nervous sweat on the palms of my hands.

What the fuck do I say? I wish I had a margarita in me.

"Thank you for coming to dinner with me, Jayden. Please forgive my sloppy behavior the other night," I said.

She laughed and replied, "No problem. It was the highlight of my night."

We started to examine the menu. We landed fajitas for two, and extra queso per Jayden's request.

"You must have queso or the fajitas are worthless," she said.

After our food arrived, we started to build our fajitas one by one. Jayden had a certain method she used that I will never forget.

She would take the tortilla and lay it flat on a small plate. Then she would smear a thick layer of queso and guacamole on the entire tortilla. Next came the refried beans, which were applied on only half of the tortilla. The other half was reserved for the rice, which she strategically placed on the opposite side of the bread foundation. After that, she crushed up a few chips and sprinkled them into the tortilla. Finally, she gently laid the fajita meat in the middle and wrapped the flour-based beast up tight. It looked like she was squeezing water out of a soaked towel.

I think I might be in love already.

I said, "Looks like you have had a lot of practice doing that."

"Are you calling me a fatty?" she said while laughing.

"No, I am calling you a genius."

We consumed the entire meal with great pleasure. I had to hand it to her. She didn't spill one piece of food on the table. I was impressed with her appetite and also with her fajita architectural skills.

I could tell that we were becoming more comfortable with each other and it felt great. She was easy to talk to, and we were both having a good time.

After dinner, we went to go see a movie at the theatre I worked at. Since it was our first movie together, I figured it was the right move to let her choose which one we saw. Jayden chose 'Monster's Inc.'

In a rather manly voice, I said, "Don't worry, Jayden, these tickets are on the house. I know people, and I'm kind of a big deal."

Jayden started to laugh and we proceeded through the lobby.

Next thing I knew, my big round boss from the theatre came up to me. She resembled a modern day Humpty Dumpty. In a raspy cigarette smoke voice, she said, "Don't be late again JUDY. You clock in at 8am sharp tomorrow. Not a minute later!"

Son-of-a-bitch.

She never got my name right, and I was so embarrassed.

Jayden said, "Don't let her get to you. I'm sure you work hard!"

"Thank you. I don't feel so bad though. She secretly squeezes the butter sauce into a small cup that she drinks throughout the day. It's only a matter of time before her heart stops," I said.

"Ha-ha. Don't say that. You're bad," Jayden replied.

We walked into the large movie theatre, and took our seats towards the back. I didn't know if this was the right time to hold her hand. I patiently waited a good twenty minutes to make sure the moment was right.

I grabbed her hand and whispered, "I'm having a great time."

She replied, "Me too. Thank you, Juddy."

Jayden put her head on my shoulder. My heart was pounding like crazy. I became nervous, and my hands began to fill up with an enormous amount of sweat. It was quite disgusting, and I knew my clammy hand would easily deter any romantic emotions.

Halfway through the movie, I went to use the restroom to cleanse my hands and urinary tract. I came back to my seat, sat down, and kept my hands to myself the rest of the movie.

After the flick was over, we headed back to Jayden's house so I could drop her off. I could sense that our hormones were slowly activating. Jayden grabbed my hand and began to scratch my arm during the ride home. As I pulled into the driveway, the house was pitch black. It looked like her parents had gone to bed.

This was my shot.

After we stepped out of the car, Jayden came over to me and gave me a hug.

"Thank so much for dinner and the movie," she said.

Jayden released her grip, and began to linger just a bit. I ducked my head underneath her eyes, and laid my greasy popcorn lips upon hers. I wanted to make sure I didn't cut her lips with my braces, so I was quite careful. I held the kiss for a while, and I was enjoying the wonderful moment.

All of a sudden, the porch light came on.

"Oh no! Did your parents see us?" I said.

I was just waiting for her father to march out there with a shotgun and blow my head off.

Jayden said, "Probably not. I think we're safe."

"Goodnight, Jayden."

"Goodnight, lover boy."

I felt on top of the world on the ride home. I rolled down the windows, cranked up some heavy metal, and hauled ass in my dad's four-cylinder sedan.

Word spread fast around school about our first date. Even though I had been somewhat victorious, I still had a long way to go. At least for now, I was the alpha male among the wolves that were hunting her at school.

The physical interest in each other started to grow rapidly, but we didn't want that to go public. We wanted our relationship to be low key. We had a few classes together, and we made sure that we never overdid it on the flirting. We would never kiss at school to avoid persecution.

Public displays of affection were strictly forbidden by the faculty...and Jesus.

Since there was no physical interaction at school, we had to go off the grid to get frisky. As teenagers it was hard to find the right time and place to be intimate. We had only scratched the surface on the physical side of things. We were both eager to explore underneath each other's clothes.

One night after we had dinner, we headed back to Jayden's house. She had been flirting with me, and kissing me all night long. Meanwhile, I couldn't keep my hands off of her. Both of us were in state of horniness. You could smell it in the air.

Towards the back of Jayden's neighborhood, there was a section of undeveloped land with empty paved streets.

I said, "I know this sounds weird, but since we really can't do anything at your parents' house, do you want to stop on one of those side streets in the back?"

Jayden replied, "I don't know. Do you think it's safe?"

My answer would seal the fate of our sexual destiny.

"Absolutely it's safe. We don't have anything to worry about."

I headed toward the back of the neighborhood. There were no streetlights up yet, and it was pitch black. At the end of one of the streets, I found an empty cul-de-sac. The cemented street would be the sacred ground on which we would explore each other's bodies for the very first time.

Since we were in the Volvo, I figured the best area for maximum pleasure would be the back seat. Instead of getting out of the car like normal people, we uncomfortably climbed to the back as if the outside air was toxic.

Once we got settled in, we began to make out…hard. We were violently tonguing one another and dry humping like jackrabbits. There was so much denim friction between our legs we could've started a small fire. The windows began to fog up, and the car was shifting back and forth. Sweat began to roll down my forehead, and I paused for a moment to crank up the AC.

We began to unbutton each other's shirts. It was the first glimpse I got of Jayden in her bra, and I was blown away. It was the first pair I'd ever seen in real life, and I couldn't take my eyes off of them. Jayden grabbed my chin and directed my eyes at her face.

"Eyes up here, mister," she said.

As we progressed, my hands eventually found their way onto Jayden's wondrous mountains. They were exquisite and supple. I then took a dive into her deep crevasse of the unknown. I explored the area for quite a bit and made a few discoveries.

Jayden had undone my belt buckle during the altercation. Her hand began to dig inside of my jeans, and was attempting to expose my first public teenaged erection.

This is it. Don't get scared now.

All of a sudden, a bright spotlight shined through the front windshield that practically blinded us. Directly above the beam of light were small multi colored flashing strobes. Either we were about to get abducted by aliens, or it was the police.

Jayden, who was scared as shit, said, "Oh my God! Hurry, get your clothes back on!"

It was a race against time and fabric. Jayden was clothed in less than five seconds, which was incredible. It was like she had been practicing on her own time. Meanwhile, I was frantically trying to fasten the buttons on my red flannel shirt. It looked like I was having a seizure.

The officer started to walk up while we were crawling over the front seats. He came up to the driver side window and said, "Roll down the window son."

"Yes, sir," I replied.

"What are you two doing out here?"

We're two horny teenagers in the backseat of a car. What the fuck you think we are doing?

"We were just talking, officer."

"I'm sure you were."

He asked for our ID's and walked back to his car to run them through his criminal database. About five minutes later, he walked over to the passenger side of the car, and asked Jayden to step out of the vehicle. He began to ask her a series of questions.

"Do you know you're sixteen, and you're in the back seat of a seventeen-year-old's car? Did he kidnap you? Are you here against your will?"

I know the officer was just doing his job, but come on, give me a break.

Jayden got back in the car, and the officer came over to me.

He said, "Now, I don't want to see you two out here again."

"Yes, sir," I said.

He let us go with a warning.

I mean really, what the hell could he have charged us with? Failure to reach climax inside a motor vehicle?

I was beginning to think that there were strange forces preventing Jayden and I from touching each other in weird places.

The six-month mark for us had arrived. I wanted to do something special for Jayden. I bought us tickets to see one of our favorite bands, Incubus. This was our first rock concert together, and we were really excited.

Jayden said, "Thank you for getting the tickets to the show. I love Incubus!"

"You're very welcome. Thank you for putting up with me for six months," I replied.

"I've had an amazing time with you!"

We took off and headed to the concert. I put on some music for the ride. Suddenly, a song came on that Jayden was quite fond of. It was by Green Day, her favorite band. The song was, 'Time of your life.'

"I love this song! Turn it up!" she said.

As I turned the silver volume knob clockwise on the stereo, I began to hear a troubling noise. It sounded like a cat getting electrocuted. It was coming out of Jayden's mouth. Attempting to suppress the blood curdling sound, I turned up the volume to full capacity. The speakers in the car were pushing the volume capacity and began to rattle.

Jayden said, "Can you turn it down?"

"I can't hear you," I said.

She grabbed the volume knob and moved it down.

"Are you trying to make us go deaf? Ha-ha."

No. Just me.

She was a straight A student, but a church choir reject.

Incubus put on an amazing show. We made out during 'Aqueous Transmission,' which was the longest song they played. It was a great experience for the both of us.

On our way home from the show, Jayden brought up something she had been hearing about from some of her girlfriends. It was a phenomenon that was sweeping the teenage nation. It had the power to increase blood flow, lower stress levels, and improve overall sleep quality. It was called, road-head.

Jayden softly said, "Do you want to try it?"

My face lit up like a damn Christmas tree.

"I would be honored," I quickly replied.

I had caught wind of this automotive oral sensation before, but I always thought it was an urban legend. I was ecstatic to embark on this new adventure that would not only test my driving skills, but also my wiener's sensation threshold.

We pulled into her neighborhood, and I gave Jayden the green light.

She said, "Just keep driving around the neighborhood, but don't go down my parents' street."

Copy that bravo leader.

It took an insane amount of concentration to operate a motor vehicle while she was operating on me. The problem was that all the blood in my brain was leaving and taking a journey to the erected statue in my pants.

My brain output level was only at about fifteen percent of its maximum potential during this time. My vision began to blur, and my basic motor skills were being affected. I was swerving in and out of lanes, and at times, scraping the side of the curb with my tires. I had driven through Jayden's neighborhood a few times before, and I knew the layout pretty well. There was however, one minor detail I forgot about. There were speed bumps scattered throughout the neighborhood like landmines. The dim streetlights barely lit up the dark pavement, so it was tough to see that night.

Before I knew it, a short glimpse of one of the large speed bumps caught my eye, but it was too late.

Brace for impact.

We struck the speed bump going about thirty, and the front two tires of my truck lifted off the ground. Jayden let out this horrible gagging sound. Instantaneously, she went completely limp like a dead animal. Her arms were draped over my legs like boiled noodles, and her head was buried in my crotch. I had never been so scared in my life. I thought I had killed her.

"Jayden! Oh my God! Jayden wake up! Are you ok?" I hysterically said.

I lifted her lifeless cranium off of me. I then propped her body up against the passenger side of the car. I began to shake her frantically, trying to wake her up. Her head was pivoting in every direction, and her tongue was hanging out. She wasn't responding, and I began to panic.

I said, "I'm sorry for doing this, Jayden."

I slapped her lightly across the face. There was no response. I slapped her again, but this time with a bit more force, like she owed me money.

Jayden instantly awoke from her temporary coma, and took a big gulp of air.

"What the hell just happened?" she asked.

What was I supposed to tell her?

I played dumb.

"Do you remember anything?" I asked.

"All I remember is that I was in the middle of, you know, doing stuff to you, and then…blackness," she replied.

"Yeah, you hit your head on the passenger side window, and you were out for a few seconds."

"Yeah my face is stinging, but my head is killing me."

After two backhanded smacks to the face, and a concussion, I figured it was time to take her home.

I said, "I'm so sorry Jayden."

"It's ok," she said. "How about we find some other place to be romantic other than the inside of your car? It's just not safe."

"I totally agree. Again, I'm very sorry."

I wonder if this shitty luck will follow me the whole way. At least there hadn't been any casualties as of yet.

Pretty soon the school year ended, and it was time for summer break. Midway through the summer, I invited Jayden over to my parents' house for dinner. They were dying to meet her, and I knew it was time.

I started to get prepped for a night of formal introductions, and I was nervous as shit. I came downstairs to help my mom with dinner. As soon as I reached the first floor, my parents started hounding me.

My mom yelled, "Did you clean up your room and the upstairs?"

"Yes, Mom," I replied.

My dad chimed in and said, "Go upstairs and put on some real clothes. You want to look presentable, not homeless."

Apparently I looked like a bum in a solid grey V-neck, shorts, and sandals. I went upstairs and put on a green polo shirt, jeans, and shoes.

About an hour later, I heard the doorbell ring.

Shit. Here goes nothing.

I rushed to the door greet Jayden.

"Hey! Come on in. Welcome to the Ferguson home," I said.

She smiled and said, "Thank You."

"Hello, Jayden, it's so nice to finally meet you. I'm Mrs. Ferguson and this is, Mr. Ferguson."

"Nice to meet you. Thank you for having me over for dinner."

"Sure, it is our pleasure."

My two younger brothers, who had been spying on us from the second story balcony, came racing down the staircase. Josh was fourteen, and Warren was ten.

After a short meet and greet, I felt more relaxed. We all sat down at the dinner table. During our meal, my mother and father bombarded Jayden with numerous questions. They were just curious, and she was polite with all of her responses.

"Juddy tells me you are quite the soccer player and very smart," my mother said.

"Yes, well, I do the best I can," Jayden replied.

Then quickly Warren blurted out, "Juddy says you're a brainiac."

I said, "Warren, shut up!"

Everyone began to chuckle, including Jayden.

After dinner, my brothers went outside to play with some kids down the street.

I asked Jayden, "Do you want to go upstairs and watch a movie?"

"Yeah, sure!" she said.

My mom had a worried look on her face. She said, "You two are going to the game room upstairs to watch a movie?"

"Yes, Mom. Is that ok?" I replied.

"Of course, but if you go in your room, leave the door open."

"Yes, ma'am."

My face turned red, and I was a little embarrassed.

We both walked upstairs into the game room. I told Jayden she could pick out the movie. She picked out one of my favorites, 'Mrs. Doubtfire.'

We curled up on the soft brown couch and started the movie.

We had some privacy, but we knew at any moment, my brothers or parents would walk up. We both hadn't been able to see each other in a few weeks, so we had some sexual tension built up.

About halfway through the movie, we started to kiss. I turned the volume up on the TV so my parents wouldn't hear the crisp smacking of our lips. The sun had gone down, and as the room became darker, our hormones became stronger.

We began to venture underneath each other's clothes, but we knew we had to keep them on as a safety measure. We had a large blanket that was used as a shield to prevent any outsiders from seeing us.

Jayden had a skirt on, so there wasn't any major obstacle's preventing me from making my way inside. Jayden on the other hand, had a tricky time with my jeans. It was like she was picking a lock. After a couple of minutes, I decided to intervene, and assist her with the copper mechanism. I was finally exposed, and Jayden grabbed a hold of my hockey stick.

She began to perform the basic top to bottom hand motion. There was a slight problem though. I could feel a sensation down under, and it was coming fast. There was fluid that had been building up inside of me since the day I hit puberty. An explosion was inevitable.

I said, "Jayden, I think something is about to happen."

"What do you mean?" she said.

"I mean…"

Before I could finish my sentence, multiple liquid projectiles launched into the air. It was like a meteor shower of embryos. Unfortunately, the point of impact was Jayden's blonde hair.

"Juddy! What the fuck?" she exclaimed.

That was the first time I heard her cuss.

"I'm so sorry, Jayden. I couldn't control it," I replied.

"My hair is going to crust if we don't wash it out!"

We both rushed into the bathroom to wash my dying children out of her hair.

"Here, use a hot damp towel to get it out," I said.

All of a sudden from downstairs, I hear my mother say, "Juddy, is everything ok up there?"

"Yes, Mom, everything is fine."

We frantically got all of the goop out. She grabbed a large towel, and after her hair was dry, she put it up in a ponytail.

"A warning would be nice next time," Jayden said.

"I'm sorry, it came out of nowhere," I replied.

We finished the rest of the movie, and then came downstairs. I walked Jayden out to her car. We both started to laugh about what had happened.

So far, our sex life had been nothing but disastrous. I couldn't help but blame myself.

"Thanks for coming over, Jayden."

"Thanks for coming 'ON' me, Juddy. Just kidding. Ha-ha!"

The summer quickly flew by and school started back up again. We had moved up one notch in the high school totem pole. We were juniors, and only one year away from graduation.

Towards the end of the fall, a big milestone arrived. It was our one-year anniversary, and it was time to celebrate.

There was an Italian place near my house that had amazing food. It was an intimate upscale restaurant, and I wanted to look sharp for her. I went into my closet and pulled out a black dress shirt, a grey tie, and my jeans. Next thing to do was to collect some anniversary supplies. I had never bought a gift for a girl before, so I went to the one place where a guy really couldn't go wrong.

The James Avery store.

I walked into the bright-lighted retail shop. It had white walls and glass cases filled with silver jewelry. I always hated shopping, and I just wanted to get the hell out of there without going flat broke.

"Just give me the necklace with the rose on it," I said.

The employee said, "Don't you want to take a closer look at it?"

"Nah. Just gift wrap the thing, and I'll be on my way."

The next stop was the grocery store for some roses. I went up to the florist counter. There was a guy in his mid-twenties that looked like he had been sucking down helium whippets in the back for hours. His eyes were droopy, and his hair looked like an old mop.

I asked, "Yes, can I have a dozen roses?"

He said, "Yeah, man. Sure thing!"

He came back out with a handful of roses. Water was dripping all over the place, and the petals were falling off. Something told me that he wasn't a florist.

"Can you wrap them up in something?" I asked.

"Oh yeah. Sorry, dude," he said.

He grabbed a piece of newspaper from the counter, and wrapped the crumpled paper around the half dead bouquet.

"Here ya go, dude," he said.

It was the most depressing set of roses I had ever seen.

"How much do I owe you?" I asked.

"It's on the house, brotha. I know how it is with lady folk. They drain your money, and then rip your heart out. I'm single now and life is so much better, dude."

"Thanks...I guess."

What if that was me in the future? Will I one day end up like him? Is that what true happiness looks like? I guess it's all in the eye of the beholder.

As I walked out of the grocery store, the newspaper wrapping began to get soggy and fall apart. I picked out the best rose out of the bunch, and just threw the rest away before I got in my car. Maybe a single rose would be more romantic.

I headed to Jayden's house to pick her up. I walked up to the front door, and rang the doorbell. Jayden answered the door, and she looked gorgeous. She was wearing a short black dress with heels. Her hair was up, and she had long silver earrings dangling down her earlobes.

"You look beautiful, Jayden," I said.

"Thank you. You look pretty dapper yourself," she replied.

Dapper? Are we in the 1920's?

We both got in the car and sitting right next to Jayden was a single red rose.

"I'm sorry. The guy at the store screwed it up. This was the best rose out of all them," I said.

"I love it, Juddy. Thank you," she replied.

I had the necklace hidden in my pocket and wanted to wait until dinner to give it to her.

The restaurant had large chandeliers hung from the ceiling. It also had dark burgundy walls and each table was covered with a black cloth and a lit candle. It was a romantic place, which included a piano player in the far corner. We were hungry and ready to order our main entrée. We picked a nice elegant dish for two. It was a good old-fashioned bowl of spaghetti and meatballs. After we ordered, I pulled out the small cardboard box out of my pocket.

I said, "I got you something, Jayden. I hope you like it. Happy Anniversary!"

Jayden said, "Thank you so much for the gift. You didn't have to buy me anything."

"It's the least I can do."

She slowly opened the box up and pulled out the necklace.

"Oh, this is so pretty, Juddy! Thank you so much!"

"It took me forever to pick out the right necklace for you."

Yeah right.

"It's perfect. Thank you for a wonderful year together, Juddy."

We began to reminisce about all of the fun and humorous moments of our relationship. We had grown tremendously over the past year, and we were very happy together. After we finished our meal, I had another surprise for her.

"Where are we going?" she asked.

I said with excitement, "I can't tell you, but it isn't too far away."

We left the restaurant and proceeded to an undisclosed location. Once we got close, I told her to close her eyes. I pulled into a dirt driveway covered in rocks. It took me about five minutes to get into the place, and then I put the car in park.

"Oh no, Juddy! We can't do this. We got busted by the cops last time," Jayden said.

I began to laugh knowing that wouldn't be the case.

"Open your eyes," I told her.

There were numerous cars scattered about the grass filled parking lot and the sun was about to go down. Sitting in front of us was a massive black screen.

"Where are we?" she asked.

I said, "At the drive-in. Tonight's feature is 'A Walk to Remember.' "

I had to take one for the team with this chick flick. Personally, I'd rather stab myself in the eye with a pencil but this had to be done.

"This is so amazing, Juddy. Thank you!" Jayden said.

We leaned our seats back, ordered some popcorn, and enjoyed the movie. This special night burned a hole right through my minimum wage salary, but I wanted to make sure it was perfect for her.

After the movie, Jayden's curfew had almost expired, so I took her home.

I walked her up to the front door of her house, and gave her a kiss

"Thank you, Juddy, for everything. I'm such a lucky girl."

"You're very welcome. Happy Anniversary, Jayden."

Chapter 2-Jayden: 'The Alcoholic Brainiac' Part 2

A new year began and things between us were at an all-time high. We didn't know quite what the future held, but we were enjoying our time together.

We resumed classes and our relationship seemed to be going steady. Although we had only been physically intimate just a few times, our hormones were firing off like a fifty caliber rifle. An inevitable question kept popping up.

When were we going take the plunge into the unknown world of sexual intercourse?

Because every other sexual encounter with Jayden was so successful...

We were two virgins just wanting to be free. Jayden seemed more eager than I did at times. She began to be more vocal about her sexual appetite. It was as if a switch had been internally activated.

"I want to do it, but I'm just scared," she said.

"Scared of what?" I asked.

"I hear that it's really painful the first time."

"I've never heard that. I only hear good things."

"I want the time to be right."

Whatever the hell that means.

A few months later, a golden opportunity presented itself. My parents were going out of town with my two brothers for a hockey tournament. We were going to have the house to ourselves for the weekend.

This is a teenage boy's dream come true. When I awake from this dream, I shall be a man that has now slain the virgin dragon.

This was the night we had been waiting for. We loved each other, and it just made sense to take the next step. I started to prepare for lift off.

I went to the grocery store to gather some supplies. The first item on my list was roses, and I grabbed a dozen. Next I found a box of vanilla scented candles to scatter all over the house. Finally, I had to purchase my very first pack of condoms, and I was nervous as shit. My hands were shaking, and I started to sweat. I headed over to the pharmacy area and found them locked in a plastic case.

Shit. Now I have to go summon a pharmacist to unlock the cabinet full of rubbers? Why the hell are they locking up something that protects you from diseases and child support?

I walked over to the pharmacy window. There was an old unsightly woman working at the counter. She had to be in her late 70's and her hair hadn't been brushed in many years.

"Yes. Hello, ma'am. Can you open the condom case for me, please?" I asked.

She looked at me with a small grin, which was creepy as hell.

"Sure, son. Just a second," she said.

She came out to the aisle and unlocked the sheath treasure chest.

"Which kind do you want?" she asked.

I grabbed the first box I saw. My hand landed on the Trojan Ultra Thins.

"These will do," I said.

"Ah yes. Those are my favorite," the wrinkled woman replied.

I think I'm going to throw up.

I stormed out of there as fast I could and rushed back home to get the house set up. I scattered rose petals in the hallway leading into my room. I also placed candles all over the house and strategically placed the condom box next to my bed. I wanted to make sure they would be easily accessible for the launch sequence. The last thing to do was to secure the food. I figured a nice 'carbo-load' couldn't hurt my chances. I ordered a lovely Olive Garden take-out dinner for the two of us.

Jayden was on her way, and I was ahead of schedule. I put on some smooth jazz music, dimmed the lights, and waited until my virgin princess arrived.

Luckily, the food showed up first. I set the table with every utensil that would be needed. I placed a tall candle in the middle of the table for ambiance. The finishing touch was two glasses of white wine, which were freshly squeezed out of a Franzia wine box.

Suddenly, the doorbell rang, and my heart started pounding. I ran up to the front door to greet Jayden.

Try to act natural, Juddy.

"Good evening, beautiful," I said.

"Why are you talking like that?" she replied while laughing at me.

"Just trying to set a romantic mood."

"It's weird."

"It's everlasting love my dear."

"Please stop."

Jayden walked into the house and saw the rose petals on the ground. She smiled at me and began to blush. I walked us into the kitchen where our bountiful feast was waiting. The food was still warm and the smell of cheese drew her in. We sat down and began to indulge in our Olive Garden pasta extravaganza. While we were eating, there was a strange feeling in the air. It was a mixture of awkwardness and anticipation. We traded seductive glances back and forth across the table like two actors at the beginning of a pornographic film. We had talked about this moment for a while, but neither one of us truly knew what to expect.

"Would you like more wine?" I asked.

"Yes, of course!" Jayden replied.

The alcohol began to enhance our romantic moods, and we were eager to finish the meal. After consuming about a pound of pasta and chicken, we made our way over to the living room to partake in more wine. In between sips, we began to kiss. My tongue was quite aggressive and quickly explored the back of Jayden's throat. It tasted like garlic.

"Let's take it slow. I want this to be special," Jayden said.

"No problem," I replied.

After four glasses of wine, we got up and began to walk down the hallway to my room. As we stepped on the rose petals, the overwhelming sexual tension that had been building up for a while began to stimulate our private parts. I was halfway to stiff-town and preparing for a close encounter with Jayden's forbidden gates.

After we entered my bedroom, I lit the candles and we started to kiss. After about five minutes, time suddenly froze. We both looked each other dead in the eyes. The time had come.

Jayden had made a mix CD for our magical journey. She filled it with various love songs for us to listen to.

"I read that music will make it more enjoyable," she said.

Once the music loaded up on the stereo, the first song came on. It was a slow love song by some shitty boy band.

I know I'm about to have intercourse with a woman for the first time in my life right now, but this is one of the gayest songs I've ever heard.

Nonetheless, we began to aggressively unclothe each other. There was a bit of foreplay, but we wanted to skip ahead to the main event. The awkward moment arose where I had to fit the small rubber balloon over my reproductive organ. I didn't realize how difficult the task would be. After a few failed attempts, I was able to securely fasten it into the upright position. We then set sail on a voyage to the land of copulation.

During the first few seconds, I was trying to get into the right position for maximum pleasure. I was moving forward, backward, left and right. I really didn't quite know what the hell I was doing, but I did my best to rock the boat.

"Does it feel good?" I asked

"Yes. It just hurts a little," she said.

"Do you want me to stop?"

"No. Keep going."

Unfortunately, I was only able to get about fifteen good thrusts in before my potency was compromised. As my seminal fluid was about to breach the surface, I immediately dislodged myself from Jayden's compartment. While I was discharging sperm at an alarming rate, I began to slowly slip into a coma. My eyes rolled into the back of my head, and I went completely limp. I had successfully initiated the preemptive ejaculation ejection protocol. I thought we were in the clear.

Suddenly, Jayden said, "Do you think I'm pregnant?"

Oh shit. Here we go.

"No. You're cool," I replied.

"I'm serious, Juddy."

"So am I."

"I guess I'm just worried. Did you go in me?"

"No. I promise."

Well, looks like I just deflowered the angel of our private Christian high school in less than five minutes. I immediately felt guilty.

God is going to shove a lightning bolt up my ass as soon as I walk out of this bedroom.

The magical moment had brought us much closer together, literally. It was an extremely short encounter, but it was very special to us. Hopefully, with practice, I could increase my lap time and prolong our future sexual endeavors. It was certainly the highlight of our summer, which was coming to an end.

It was finally our last year in high school. We both focused our attention on academics more than anything. Studying became our main priority. We attended study halls together and did a lot of after school studying at the public library.

A few months into the school year, the first senior party was being formulated. Jayden and I wanted to attend because we hadn't been out in awhile, and we wanted to socialize.

All the seniors pitched in money to buy alcohol for the party. On the list was: two kegs of Bud Light, two dozen handles of various liquors, and for some reason, Smirnoff Ice.

Any guy caught drinking one of those would surely get his ass kicked.

Unfortunately, Jayden had an early soccer game scheduled the morning after the party. Her parents wanted her home early to rest up because there were going to be college scouts attending the game. She had to be home by 10pm and no later.

A few days later, we headed out to the party. We arrived and the street was jam packed with cars. We could hear the rap music blaring from six houses down. We walked up the driveway towards the backyard. As we came up to the garage, there was a group of people playing beer pong along with a few guys doing keg stands. We said hello to everyone and headed inside.

There was a large crowd in the kitchen area which was covered in stainless steel appliances. There were plastic cups scattered all over the floor and excess beer spilling off the countertops. The house was filled with drunks from wall to wall, and it looked like the party started hours ago.

Jayden immediately darted over to her girlfriends while I grabbed some drinks. I found Nick, the MC for the party, who happened to be a good friend of mine.

He said, "Juddy! My man! How are you, buddy?"

"Hey, dude! Thanks for throwing the party!" I said.

"Hell yeah, man! I have a surprise for you."

Nick guided me over to his large kitchen oven. Sitting inside were four trays of weed brownies baking at 350 degrees.

"They're almost done," he said.

Ten minutes later, Nick grabbed the trays out of the oven. The steam coming off the top of the dark brown crusted squares had a fresh mint aroma. He set the trays down on the countertop and everyone started to dig in like vultures on a dead carcass. I grabbed what looked like two solid pieces. Apparently, I was not the best at sizing food portions. I accidentally inhaled a total of eight weed brownies in two minutes.

With chocolate residue on my cheeks, I went looking for Jayden. I hadn't seen her the entire party, and it was almost time to head back home. I looked around in the backyard for her. All I saw were a couple of passed out drunks scattered on the wooden deck.

I went back inside to search more. All of a sudden, the brownies began to take effect on my brain. Everything looked like it was in slow motion. I made my way to the staircase at the front of the house. It had transformed into an elevated footpath of astronomical proportions. It looked like the stairway to heaven and at the top there were white clouds.

As I embarked on my upward journey, every step up I took, another step would appear at the top. It was a never-ending fucking staircase.

After what felt like an eternity, I finally made it to the top. There was a long empty hallway with about five bedrooms. I overheard

Jayden's voice about two doors down. I went up to the door and busted it wide open like I was serving a search warrant.

Jayden was laying down in bed with her friend Ashley and some random guy who had his head on Jayden's lap.

"Hey there. Remember me? Your boyfriend?" I asked.

"Juddy, calm down. I'll be outside in a minute," Jayden replied in frustration.

"No problem. I'll wait right here."

"Ugh fine. I have to go, guys."

Jayden walked out of the room. Her two bed buddies were giggling in the background.

"What the hell was that all about?" I asked.

"Nothing. We were just hanging out," she said.

"Whatever. Let's get out of here."

I grabbed Jayden's hand to take her downstairs. The staircase began to move from left to right like an old wooden jungle bridge from Indian Jones. Underneath it was hot lava and it scared the shit out of me. I was beginning to think that these brownies were laced with something other than marijuana. Stage two of the weed brownie trip was now in progress

"Hold on to the rails! I don't want you to fall!" I exclaimed.

"What the hell is wrong with you?" she asked.

"Dammit, woman! Just do what I say!"

I guided Jayden down the stairs like an elderly woman. It took us quite some time, but I had to make sure we stayed alive. We walked outside, and I was trying to recall not only where I parked, but also what type of car I came in. I started to walk aimlessly down the street. Jayden grabbed my arm and said, "You parked your truck over here, dummy!"

I turned around and there I saw my trusty red truck shining bright underneath a streetlight a few houses down. Before we got in the vehicle, I stopped Jayden and said, "Can you drive? I'm not feeling so well."

"Why?" she asked.

"I just don't feel good."

During the ride home, phase three of the weed brownie trip went into effect. It looked like we were going turbo speed in a video game. The streetlights were flying past the window like stars during warp speed.

"Jayden, you're going too fast! Slow down...PLEASE!" I said.

"What are you talking about? I'm going the speed limit," she replied in annoyance.

I turned my head to look over at Jayden. Her nose had grown about nine inches and was almost touching the windshield. She also had goblin ears like Yoda, and for some reason, her breath smelled terrible. Every time she spoke, a gust of rank wind passed over my frightened face.

What the fuck was in those brownies?

"What are you staring at?" she said.

"Jayden, I'm going to ask you a serious question," I said.

"Um, ok."

"Has your nose grown recently?"

"Are you serious? You are such an asshole!"

We pulled up into the driveway of Jayden's house twenty minutes later. I was thinking about giving her a kiss goodbye, but her dragon breath was burning my nostrils.

"I'm so pissed at you," she said.

"I know. I'm sorry for asking that," I replied.

"Are you ok to drive home?"

"Yeah. I think so."

"We will talk about this tomorrow. Be safe and don't be a moron."

I hopped over into the driver's seat. My senses were working at full capacity, and I was completely relaxed. I had never driven under the influence, but I wanted to sleep in my own bed that night.

I pulled into my parent's driveway, and slowly made my way to the front door. I quietly snuck my way in and ran upstairs as fast as I could. I walked into my room and the white comforter on my bed looked like a huge pile of marshmallows. I dove into the bed like an Olympic swimmer at the start of a race. As soon as my face hit the soft surface, it was lights out.

The next day I woke up around 11am. It was the best damn sleep I'd ever had. I felt refreshed, rejuvenated, and ready to take on the world. That positive rush quickly lost steam after I looked over at my phone and noticed a barrage of text messages from my girlfriend.

"Did you make it home? Where are you? Call me now!" the messages read.

I quickly called her to let her know I was ok. She was still pissed, but she was glad I made it home safe.

"Jayden, why were you in bed with Ashley and some random guy?" I asked.

"We were just hanging out and taking shots," she replied.

"Why was the guy's head on your lap?"

"It was nothing, Juddy. It was just a guy I met there. You don't have any room to talk. What did you take last night?"

"I just ate some really good brownies."

"I'm sure you did. I guess we're even."

Even though she had a point, I still had my doubts. She didn't interact with me the entire time at the party. Maybe my braces were hindering my sex appeal, and she was losing interest in me.

I walked downstairs after I got off the phone. My mother was waiting for me in the kitchen. As soon as my feet touched the tile floor, she asked, "Did you have fun last night?"

"Yeah I did. Why?" I asked.

"Your truck is parked on our front lawn for some stupid reason."

Oh shit.

I looked out the front door. I had destroyed the flower garden in the middle of the lawn and also put three-foot divots in the grass.

"You're grounded," she said.

"I know," I replied.

Right before Christmas break, it was finals time. Jayden academically exempted out of most of her finals, so she was able to help me study for mine. We would go to the library after school, load up on Starbucks coffee, and quiz each other until the place closed.

During study breaks at the library, our future began to surface in conversation.

"What do you think will happen to us?" Jayden said.

"What would you like to happen?" I asked.

"I would like to stay together, but we could end up in different states."

"I'm willing to make it work. I love you, Jayden."

"I love you too, Juddy. I just hope we are close enough to visit each other."

Jayden already had scholarship offers from over a dozen schools all over the country. Meanwhile I had already been planning on going to a state college not too far from town.

A few weeks later, she revealed to me that she had narrowed her choices down to about four different schools. Two of them were a thousand miles away. The other two were only about four hours away.

"Where do you want to go?" I asked.

"I don't know. I like them all," she said.

We both left the discussion open ended and nothing was really accomplished in the search for an answer to our future. It almost felt that we were avoiding the issue and just living for the moment.

After the New Year began, Jayden was getting ready to fly out to an honors retreat in Washington D.C. She had been selected by the faculty to represent our high school. It was a two-week-long leadership program to prepare students for college. It was our last weekend together before she left, and she invited me over to her house for the night. When I arrived, I joined Jayden and her parents for dinner. Afterwards, Jayden and I went upstairs to watch some TV.

After we got settled on the couch, Jayden said, "Hey, I want to talk to you about something."

"Yeah. Sure," I said.

"I really want us to make it. I want us to be together. The only way to do that is to be as close as we can after high school."

"I want to be with you too, Jayden, but I thought you wanted to go out of state?"

"I want to be close to home and close to you."

"You don't have to do this just because of me. I just want you to be happy."

"The college offered me a full scholarship, and you will only be a few hours away."

I was excited about Jayden's collegiate choice, but I knew a long-distance relationship would be a tough road. I was prepared to make it work and drive up as much as I could to visit her. It seemed that both of us were committed to the relationship and we were on the same page.

That following Monday, Jayden flew away to D.C. for her training. Part of me felt like a free man, but the other half felt like something was missing. Our two-year anniversary was coming up in a few days, and I wanted to send her something while she was on her trip. I called her mom to obtain the hotel and room number Jayden was staying in. I ordered a dozen roses with some nice chocolates to be delivered to her room. Included in the care package was a note that read, "Happy Anniversary Jayden. Here's to many more together. Have a good time in D.C. I'm so proud of you. Love, Juddy."

Jayden called me early the very next day.

"Thank you so much for the flowers and chocolates. I love you, and I can't wait to see you when I get back," she said.

"You're very welcome! I'll see you soon. I love you," I replied.

The remainder of her two-week training convention, I didn't hear a single peep from her. Not a phone call, text message, or anything. Maybe she was busy at the geek convention solving math problems and stroking test tubes.

A few days later, Jayden arrived back home on a Sunday morning. She didn't call me until later that night.

"Hey! I made it home safe and sound," she said.

"I'm so glad you're back. I missed you," I told her.

"Uh huh. Me too."

"Ok well, I can't wait to see you at school tomorrow!"

"Yeah! See you tomorrow!"

That was strange.

The next day, I got to school earlier than usual so I could spend some time with her before the 8am bell rang. I was anxiously sitting in the cafeteria hall not really knowing what to expect. She walked in a few minutes later. She had a smile on her face and came up to give me a hug. It felt good holding her again.

"I missed you, Jayden!"

"I missed you too!"

So far, so good.

She had a big pink photo binder in her arms.

"I want to show you everything I did on the trip!" she eagerly said.

"Yes of course. We have plenty of time before class," I told her.

Most of the pictures were with the girls that were in her group in various locations around the capital. There were field trips during the day and social events at night. As she was flipping the crisp laminated papers, she skipped through about six pages right in the middle.

I stopped her from going any further.

"Wait. Go back to the middle. I want to see everything," I said.

She was hesitant at first.

"Ok. These were the boring social events," she said.

As she flipped back to the middle pages, multiple pictures surfaced of some guy hanging all over her. There was even one picture of this douchebag kissing her on the cheek.

"What the hell is this?" I asked.

"Don't freak out. He was just a friend," she replied.

"Well it sure looks like a lot more than that."

"Look if I cheated on you, I would just tell you."

"Thanks for the honesty. I feel so much better now."

"I had fun on this trip, and that's all that mattered."

The bell rang and we both headed to class. I was in shock about her remarks. This wasn't the girl I knew.

All of a sudden, Jayden began to change.

Her ego began to grow at an exponential rate. Jayden always knew she could get any guy she wanted at school. She used this to her advantage to gain an edge over me. She began to flirt back and forth with other guys. It was nothing serious, but it was just enough to make me feel like an idiot. She knew she had my attention, and she knew I was the weaker one due to my highly emotional personality.

I was upset with the way she was acting. Surely, her love for me had not vanished. I needed to let her know how serious I was about us. I also needed to break her out of this ego trip.

Instead of instigating a fight between us, I decided to take a different approach. I wanted to prove my love for her rather than argue. I felt it was the right thing to do.

Prom was right around the corner, and I wanted to ask Jayden in a very special way. The school's annual talent show was coming up in a few weeks, and I knew I could use the event to my advantage.

A week before the show, I met with the captain of the drill team. She was a good friend of mine named Candice who graciously agreed to help me. The drill team was already planning on performing a dance midway through the talent show. After the performance, the team was going to help me ask Jayden to prom in front of everyone.

It was the day of the show, and I drove over to Jayden's house to pick her up.

"Are you excited for the show?" I asked.

"Yeah. Thanks for picking me up!" she replied.

"There are some last minute talent show spots to fill if you want to get up there and sing. Ha-ha."

"I wouldn't be caught dead on stage, and why is that so funny?"

"Oh, no reason."

When we walked inside the school cafeteria, there were about 250 people in the crowd. It was a bit overwhelming, and I started to get nervous. I wanted to make sure we had a good view, so I picked seats in the center isle about twenty feet away from the stage.

About halfway through the show, the drill team was set to perform. They did an 80's dance melody which was pretty entertaining. The crowd started to cheer after the performance was over. The drill team then exited off the stage. There was a ten second moment of silence, and the hair on the back of my neck stood up.

Candice came back on stage, grabbed the microphone and said, "Excuse me, everyone, the drill team has a very special announcement to make."

Everyone in the crowd was confused and filled with anticipation. The drill team walked back out onto the stage. Each member had a green cardboard sign in their hands with the blank side facing the audience. One by one from left to right, the members of the drill team flipped over each sign which revealed: "JAYDEN, WILL YOU GO TO PROM WITH ME? -JUDDY."

Jayden gasped as if she had seen a ghost. Everyone in the crowd was shifting around in their seats trying to find us. Jayden turned bright red and covered her face with her hands. I wrapped my arms around her and squeezed tight. Everyone began to clap and cheer for us.

"Is that a yes?" I asked.

She didn't even say a word. She just nodded her head while still covering her embarrassed face. Then she wrapped her arms around me. It was one of the best moments of our relationship, but unfortunately, the act of compassion was soon despaired.

About a week before prom, something strange happened.

Jayden started to become very distant at school. She would avoid me in the hallways, and whenever we did converse, she started to bring up the idea of breaking up, which absolutely devastated me.

"Long-distance relationships never work. We should just break up now, so we can have the summer to ourselves," she said.

"What are you talking about? I thought we loved each other and that we were going to make it work?" I pleaded.

"Why can't we just break up now and have fun before we go to college?"

"Why do you want to break up? What did I do wrong? I thought we loved each other?"

"I don't know anymore. I'm just confused about what I want right now."

My heart dropped to the ground. I didn't know what to do. We both had many memories together, and there was no reason to throw away everything we had worked for. I was willing to do anything to win her affection back. I wanted us to survive.

I went through the next couple of days walking on eggshells wondering what was going to happen next. My stress level rose tremendously, and I was having trouble sleeping. Everything we had was about to be erased from history, never to be seen again.

On the inside, I was heartbroken and living in fear. On the outside, it was business as usual. We remained together, but there was a good chance that she would eventually label me as a lost cause. It was an unhealthy way to live, but I believed we were meant to be together.

Senior prom came and I really didn't know what to expect. This would be an awkward night for the both us. Nevertheless, I put on my suit and tie and drove to pick Jayden up.

She had on a red dress with silver trim surrounding it. It was backless and had a low cut top in the front. It was exotic looking, almost like a Japanese kimono dress. She looked magnificent, and that killed me a little bit inside.

"You look absolutely beautiful," I said

"Thank you, Juddy. Are you ready?" she asked.

"I guess so."

"Let's just get through tonight and see what happens."

We drove to the high school to drop off my car and meet up with our group of friends. A few minutes later, a limo picked us up and took us to dinner. We mingled with our friends like everything was normal. We held hands, kissed each other, but it just felt artificial. I kept smiling and pretended like everything was ok.

I had snuck a flask of vodka for the road. I made drinks for Jayden and me on the car ride back to the dance. Maybe if she had some alcohol in her veins, she would loosen up a bit.

We both finished off the flask before we got to the dance. Everyone in the limo drunkenly filed out onto the pavement at school. Some of the people in our group had trouble standing, but we managed to drag ourselves into our last high school dance.

Jayden and I went out on the dance floor a few times. We mostly danced to the slow songs and there wasn't too much communication between us. About two hours in, the announcement came for the prom king and queen. Jayden was nominated, and I knew she wanted to win it. She always had a competitive spirit.

Unfortunately, she did not win. She was beaten by one of our good friends, Amanda.

"I'm sorry you didn't win. You are definitely the prettiest girl here; that is for sure," I said.

"Thanks. I just want to leave. Can we get out of here?" she sadly asked.

"We sure can."

Our next stop was Project Prom, which was held directly after the dance. It was essentially a non-alcoholic abstinence party used as a lock-in blockade to stop students from having fun. We were to be held there as prisoners until five in the morning. Jayden was required to go by her mother, so of course, I also had to suffer. I couldn't think of a worse way to end my senior year.

There was a moonwalk, bingo, karaoke, and video games. It was the perfect setup for a bunch of fifth graders. They should've just added a finger-painting station and a clown.

Lord, kill me now.

During our time there, we mostly played bingo because there were prizes involved. We won some gift certificates, a George Foreman grill, and a few other things. It was actually the first time I saw Jayden smile that night. She looked happy.

Once the greatest party on earth was over the sun began to rise. We hopped in my truck to head home. My brain was fried from the lack of sleep, and as soon as I dropped Jayden off I went home and crashed.

We marched forward with our relationship, even though I was still in doubt. I was angry she couldn't give me any answers. Each day was a battle trying to stay together, and I was beginning to feel helpless.

A week later, graduation had finally come. The ceremony was held at a large church down the street from our high school. It was a big moment for us, and a milestone we were ready to cross. There were only about 130 graduates, so the service was only about an hour long.

Jayden received the salutatorian award being second ranked in the class, meanwhile I was just happy that the speaker pronounced my name correctly. After it was over, we met with our parents for pictures, and then headed to a few graduation parties.

Jayden had accepted a full academic scholarship to the school she had as her first choice. She was also invited to play on the school's soccer team as a starter.

I had been accepted into a state college that was close to home. I was invited to play on the hockey team for the college as well.

Jayden had a strict training schedule she had to adhere to in order to be ready for the soccer season in the fall. This meant running in the early morning fog, scorching hot afternoon sprints, and late night cardio every day of the week. It was the ultimate recipe for the shittiest summer ever recorded.

Instead of hanging out by the pool with my friends, which would've been awesome, I dedicated myself to Jayden. I trained with her in order to help her prepare for her first collegiate soccer season. I wanted to spend as much time as I could with her before we left for college. Maybe if she saw my dedication, she would once again find the love she had for me. I sucked it up, never complained, and did it all for her.

With all the training we were doing, I was always exhausted at work. My sleep schedule was all jacked up. I would work late, wake up early to get my ass kicked with Jayden, and then slowly die in the afternoon. We never really had time to go out on dates so the time we had training I valued quite a bit.

After a solid two months of training, the summer was coming to an end. Jayden invited me over to her house one night for dinner and a movie. It seemed to be just like any other night.

When I arrived, Jayden was in a weird melancholy mood. She hesitated looking me in the eyes, and she was talking very softly to me. It was as if she was hiding something.

"Come in, Juddy. Join us for dinner," she said.

Is this the last supper?

There was an awkward silence at the dinner table, as if everyone knew something that I didn't. I tried to start up a conversation, but it didn't go anywhere.

After dinner Jayden and I went upstairs to watch a movie. She put on the 'Mighty Ducks.'

Uh oh. She's buttering me up with one of my favorite movies. This can't be good.

About ten minutes into the movie, she said, "Juddy, I need to talk to you about something."

"Ok," I hesitantly replied.

"Juddy, I love you and I always will. You have made me very happy during the time we have had together. You have been an amazing boyfriend. I'm just not 'in love' with you anymore. I think it would be best if we broke up before we left for college, so we can start a new chapter in our lives. A long-distance relationship will never work between us."

"WHY you are not 'in love' with me anymore?"

"I don't know. This isn't easy for me, Juddy."

"It was never easy for me. I was the one fighting for us. I was the one that tried to hold us together, but all you wanted to do is rip us apart."

"This is for the best. For both of us."

"You have not been the same since your trip to D.C."

"What are you talking about?"

"You know exactly what I'm talking about."

"I really don't, Juddy."

"If you haven't figured that out by now, you never will."

I was filled with rage and sadness. I quickly made my way out the front door without saying another word. I tried to hold back my tears while racing down the empty staircase. Once I was outside, there was a torrential downpour running down my cheeks. Tears were sliding down my face faster than I could run, and snot was pouring out of my nose like a waterfall.

As I was getting in my car, Jayden came outside. She called out to me in a distressed voice. I wanted to turn back so badly, but I had to go.

I sped off into the night and never looked back.

When I got back home I ran into my room and started to cry. I was so hurt and so confused. I was engulfed in the flames of anger for many days. I didn't talk to anyone and kept my feelings hidden from the outside world. I fell into a depressive hibernation for the rest of the summer.

Chapter 3-Jayden: 'The Alcoholic Brainiac' Part 3

Communication did not exist between us after that night. I was confused, torn, and emotionally exhausted. I was broken inside, and the memories of us began to fade into dust as the days went by. I didn't want to hold onto anything that reminded me of her. Photos, cards, and love notes were destroyed. After I purged myself of the ex-girlfriend, I had to prepare myself for a new beginning. It was the dawn of frat parties, hangovers, and bad decisions. I was ready to embrace college life for the very first time.

Luckily, my good friend, John, from high school happened to be going to the same college and we signed up as roommates. Unfortunately, we registered a little too late. We were assigned to the most run down dormitory on campus. It was called King Hall or simply 'The Slums.'

It was a red brick six-story building that had been constructed in the dark ages of the eighteenth century. There were green spots all over the walls and empty beer cans scattered all over the lawn. Every student we saw walking into the dorm looked depressed. It was like a commune for the rejects and this was the point of no return.

The inside smelled like a wet foot, and the carpet was covered in dark brown stains. This was going to be my new home, and I could hardly wait to set up base camp.

We had a nice freshman bachelor pad, which included a small TV complete with an aluminum antenna, a mini-fridge, and a year supply of Ramen noodles.

Once classes started, we decided to join the largest fraternity on campus called Sigma Chi. We were both given bids to join, and we were ready to party. We then began a long six-month pledge-ship shortly after rush week. We were excited to join the Greek life, but little did we know we had just sold ourselves into slavery.

Being a pledge sucked, but at least it kept my mind off Jayden. We had to be at the frat house at 6am every morning. We either got our balls rocked by the brothers or had to clean the entire garbage infested shithole for an hour. We also had to wear white T-shirts that were tucked into our jeans anytime we were on campus or at the frat house. Our pledge book was to be with us at all times, and we had to formally greet every active fraternity member on campus. It was like we were a bunch of Mormons without bike helmets.

Jayden had begun college as well, and she had a tough class schedule. She was taking eighteen hours, while I was only taking twelve. On top of that, she began her brutal soccer training to get ready for the season opener. She was very busy trying to manage her schedule.

Unfortunately, Jayden began to tread down a dangerous path about three months into her college career.

She was finally free from her strict parents. It was like releasing an animal into the wild after being caged for eighteen years. The alcoholic floodgates had burst wide open. She began to drink heavily and shortly thereafter, the drunk-dialing began.

The first few calls were very late at night; two, three, even four in the morning. I would wake up and find multiple voicemails on my phone. The collection of belligerent dialogue started to fill up my inbox rapidly. I started to check the messages one by one. Most of them I really couldn't make out any words. It was sloppy, mumbled, and slow the whole way through. I never knew what alien language she was speaking in.

Then one night, she managed to call me at a reasonable hour. I picked up the phone preparing myself for another episode of three sheets to the wind starring Jayden Matthews.

"Hello, Jayden. How are you?" I asked.

"Hello, lover boy. I'm doing just fucking dandy," she said.

Oh shit.

"Well that sounds…fun."

"I want to tell you something."

"Ok."

"I miss you."

"Alright."

"Aren't you going say anything?"

"Nope."

"Fuck you then. We are over!"

She hung up the phone.

Well, that was delightful.

I didn't hear from her for a few days, but like clockwork, she called again. I hesitated to take the call, but maybe she needed help. When I answered, I could practically smell the vodka seeping through the speaker of the phone.

"I'm sorry I broke your heart. I was just confused at the time. I didn't know how important you were to me until I broke up with you," she said.

"That…really doesn't make me feel any better," I replied while laughing.

"You think this is funny? I am exposing my feelings and all you do is laugh?"

"What do you want me to say?"

"I want you to say that you love me."

"What if I don't anymore?"

"Then we are done here."

She hung up the phone.

It was as if Jayden had completely forgotten everything that happened between us in high school. She was the one who destroyed us and that will never be undone. The feelings I once had for her had already disappeared.

After that night, Jayden's life began to crumble.

During her first year of collegiate soccer, she practiced hard, but never played in a single game during the season…not even for a minute. She thought for sure she would get some playing time on the field. She was not accustomed to being benched. Jayden was a talented player, who always started first on the field when she played back home. The lack of participation was an insult, and it took quite a toll on her. It caused her heavy drinking to get worse, and the drunken calls to return.

Her voice had the texture of a Sloppy Joe. She would smash all of her words together, and it sounded like the sentences were slowly pouring from her mouth.

"Heyyyyyy, whaaaaat are you dooooooing?" she asked.

"Trying to get some sleep. I have to be at the frat house at 6am," I said.

"Whateverrrrr. So, do youuu still love me?"

"As a friend, yes I do."

Friend-zone activated.

"Are youuuuuu serious? Only as a friend?"

"Yes."

"Fine, whatever. Don't ever call me again."

"Uh. Ok then."

Once again, she hung up the phone with brute force.

Another wall that was crashing down was Jayden's academic performance. She was now making straight C's in every class. Her academic scholarship was in jeopardy, and things were getting worse.

The late night calls from Jayden slowly began to fade away. It would be one call a night then two calls per week. Then towards the end of the semester, they stopped completely.

Weeks started to go by and there were no signs of life. After a month of silence, I became worried.

Where did she go? Was she safe?

I started to reach out to her on the phone. For two weeks, the calls went straight to voicemail like her phone had been turned off. Then one day, I received one of the strangest calls of my life. It came from Jayden's mother.

She said, "Hello, Juddy. I have something I need to tell you. Jayden has checked into the psychiatric hospital. She had a severe depressive episode."

"Oh my God. Is she ok?" I asked.

"She is ok, but she is not talking to her father or myself. She told the doctor that you are the only one she will speak to. I need you to come up here please and help us."

Why me? I'm nothing. These were her parents...her family.

"I'll leave right now. I should be there in four hours," I said.

"Please hurry," her mother begged.

I started to frantically pack my things before I hit the road. I threw whatever I could into my small duffle bag. Within ten minutes, I got in my car and hauled ass. As I was driving, the shadow of guilt began to surround me like a bad thunderstorm.

Was this my fault?

After a long drive, I arrived at the hospital. It was a large off white facility with a big iron gate at the front entrance. I pulled up to the security guard booth to sign in. The guard directed me to the visitor parking lot, and I quickly found a spot.

It was dark already, and the lights in the parking lot were very dim.

I found my way to the front entrance of the hospital, took a deep breath, and walked in.

Inside the lobby there was old wooden furniture covered in dust. There was outdated wallpaper, and a certain musty smell that could only be described as sadness. The front desk was located towards the back of the lobby. Behind it, was a caged area that had restricted access signs on it. I nervously walked up to the secretary.

"Last name?" she said in an old raspy voice.

"Ferguson, ma'am," I replied.

She looked through her binder of ruffled papers. She then stopped and glanced at me with a look of nervousness.

"Standby, Mr. Ferguson."

She pushed a red button that was on top of her desk. The buzzer sounded like the end of a basketball game in an old gymnasium. It was loud, foggy, and obnoxious. Two large male guards in all white uniforms came from behind the desk. They had padded handcuffs in their hands.

"I think there's been a mistake," I said.

"Calm down, Mr. Ferguson. We don't want any trouble," one of the guards said.

"My name is, Juddy Ferguson. I am here to visit a patient named, Jayden Matthews."

One of the guards grabbed my arm.

"Don't struggle, Mr. Ferguson," he said.

The secretary then intervened.

She said, "Wait. We have the wrong Ferguson. The patient that is being admitted today is, Thomas Ferguson. Let him go guards. Sorry, sir. Right this way."

I've only been in this fucking place for five minutes and was about to be locked away in a padded room.

The secretary guided me to the visitor center. As I walked around the corner into the lounge area, I saw Jayden's parents. Her father had his arms wrapped around Jayden's mother. It looked like she had been crying for a while.

I said, "Hello, Mr. and Mrs. Matthews. I'm so sorry for what happened to Jayden. How is she?"

"She is in a private room down the hall with the doctor. She only wants to talk to you," her mother said.

"I will go talk to her as soon as she is ready."

My hands began to shake. I was not prepared for this whatsoever, but I knew it had to be done. Ten minutes later, the doctor walked through the door. He asked me if I would meet with Jayden privately. I agreed to do so, and he guided me down the long hallway to her room.

Passing by the metal doors one by one, I felt an extreme amount of fear. The air was cold and my nerves were twitching. I didn't know what to expect. I wasn't sure if I could handle the pressure of walking into an enclosed area with her.

I came upon the room where Jayden was being kept. I looked through the front window. She was lying down on a steel framed bed, face up, staring at the ceiling. Her hair was frizzy, and her skin was pale. She also looked like she had lost some weight.

The doctor opened the door, and I slowly walked in. Jayden quickly rose up from the bed like the possessed girl in 'The Exorcist.' I took a seat next to her.

"Jayden, are you ok? What happened?" I asked.

"You left me all alone," she hissed at me.

"What do you mean?"

"I needed you, and you weren't there."

"I don't understand."

"Why don't you love me anymore?"

"You broke up with me, remember?"

"Yes, but I love you. I've always loved you, and you deserted me."

"I'm here for you now, Jayden. I want to help you."

"I'm in this fucking place…because of you."

Jayden had placed the blame on me for her breakdown, which caused me to feel an overwhelming amount of anger. Why was she pointing the barrel of the gun at me? What really happened that night she checked in here? I didn't dare ask that question. Maybe I was better off not knowing.

After Jayden condemned me of my wicked ways, I was speechless. There was a cloud of awkwardness growing inside the room.

Jayden demanded, "I want to see my parents now!"

I said, "Ok. I'll go get them.

I walked out of the room feeling like an asshole. I didn't know where to go from here, and I was fearful of Jayden's mental condition.

I stayed in close contact with Jayden during the following days of her episode. We were on the phone four times a day. She slowly began to come back to reality, and each day got better.

A week later, the hospital released Jayden back into the world. She resumed her college classes, but still attended therapy sessions three times a week at the hospital.

Right before school let out for the winter break, Jayden invited me to 'bring a friend day' at the hospital. The event consisted of about twenty-five patients, their guests, and one lead speaker. I wanted to help, so I agreed to attend. I quickly packed my things and drove up to meet Jayden.

In the back of my mind, I felt like I was being setup. If Jayden had blamed me for everything that happened to her, then I guess this meeting could very well be my crucifixion.

When I arrived at Jayden's dorm room, there was a strange feeling in the air. I didn't quite know how Jayden felt about me. She had been pretty nice to me on the phone, but I had my doubts. Who knows what kind of hatred was within her? I knew at any moment, she might snap, and snatch the soul of my body.

When we arrived at the hospital, Jayden and I walked upstairs to a big room with white walls, vomit colored carpet, and barred windows. There were old steel chairs that were set up in a large circle. There were fifty to sixty people there for the gathering of troubled minds.

The lead speaker told us to take our seats, and the therapy session began. He was an older fellow, and his name was Greg.

He said, "Hello, friends and family. Thank you for joining us on this special day. I want to tell you about why I'm here."

Greg began to reveal his horrific back-story. When he was nine, Greg was being bullied by two teenage boys on a regular basis. The bullying escalated one day after school. The two boys kidnapped

Greg from the bus stop and took him to a remote cabin in the woods. The two teenagers sexually abused Greg for hours and then left him there. Beaten and broken inside, Greg eventually made his way home to tell his parents what had happened. Thankfully, the two pieces of shit were arrested and charged. The pain he must have gone through…I couldn't even imagine nor comprehend.

After Greg spoke, the magnitude of Jayden's unfortunate episode began to sink in. The other patients began opening up one by one about their addictions and vices. Most of them had been abused or addicted to drugs at one point in their life. Jayden declined to speak during the session which I found odd.

I was staring across a crowded room looking at people who had been to hell and back.

Even though I had a large amount of sympathy for all of the patients, Jayden's tragic story had me conflicted.

She was blessed with the opportunity to attend a prestigious school, but decided to party hard instead. Her life then began to collapse at an alarming rate, and she didn't know how to control it. I don't blame her for breaking down, but Jayden failed to take responsibility for her own mistakes. In her eyes, I was the one at fault for her shitty grades, heavy drinking, and depression.

Jayden didn't want to admit to her parents, who held her in a very high regard, that she had made numerous mistakes. These mistakes caused a negative ripple effect on her entire collegiate career. She was close to having the scholarship ripped from her fingers, and she decided to make me her whipping boy. That was her way out to make sure she kept her parents happy and to justify her problems at hand.

Towards the end of the group session, Greg asked all of the patients to take out their personal journals. He began to tell us that these journals were meant to record the thoughts and struggles that the patients were facing at the time. Jayden was very reluctant to pull out her journal. I soon realized that she wanted to make sure I never saw a word of it. I could only imagine the horrible picture she must have painted of me on the inside of that paper bound book.

After the session was over, I was disoriented to say the least. I didn't quite understand why Jayden wanted me there in the first place. I guess she wanted to inject me with guilt, so that I would show her compassion.

We went back to her dorm room and dove right into a deep emotional conversation.

Jayden had it embedded in her mind that in order to fix everything, we should get back together.

She said, "It all went wrong when we broke up. It only makes sense to get back together."

I said, "Why should I get back with someone who blamed me for everything?"

"I know it was all my fault, but I believe we belong together."

"I don't know if getting back together is going to fix any of this."

Jayden became angry.

"Do you want to know what happened that night I broke down? I was rushed to the hospital because I had overdosed on Vicodin. My heart rate dropped so low, that it almost stopped beating. Do you want me to do that again?" she asked.

I replied, "My God, no. Why would you do that to yourself?"

This revelation scared the ever-living shit out of me. I was faced with a very difficult decision. If something were to happen to her, I could never live with myself.

Sometimes you really don't understand the reckless decisions that you make under pressure. We tend to act before speaking or more importantly, before thinking. Maybe I'm just one gullible motherfucker.

"I don't want to see any harm come to you. If you need me to be with you in order to help you, then I will," I said.

I knew in my heart that I was not in love with her anymore, but the blame that she so graciously bestowed upon me was staggering. I wanted to back out. I wanted to leave her, but I was fearful for her life.

Jayden had twisted her downfalls around to make me look like the bad guy, which I knew I wasn't. Ironically, I felt it was my duty to be there and to help her get back on her feet. I knew the relationship wouldn't last, but I was trying to do best thing for her without thinking of myself.

The next semester of college was tough. I was struggling to maintain my grades and keep up with the rejuvenated long-distance relationship. I was talking to Jayden on the phone everyday for at least an hour. The conversations were extremely boring and monotonous. She kept repeating the same shit over and over.

She would ask me questions like, "Do you still love me?"

I would always answer yes. I felt sorry for her. I wasn't being honest, and I knew that it would eventually catch up to me and bite me in the ass.

"I'm not doing so well. Can you come up and see me?" she asked one day.

"Yes. I'll leave tomorrow after my classes are over," I reluctantly replied.

I headed out on Friday afternoon. The drive to Jayden's college always sucked. There was no scenery whatsoever. All I saw were RV parks, gas stations, and XXX stores.

Once I got in town, I headed over to pick Jayden up from her dorm. Since her dormitory was 'girls only,' we were going to have to find another place to crash for the night.

"Hey, lover boy. How are you?" she said.

"I'm exhausted and hungry," I replied.

"Aren't you happy to see me?"

"Yes. I am"

Kind of.

We took a short drive to a café in town. Once we sat down, Jayden began to catch me up on current events. She had been doing much better in school, cut down on her drinking, and seemed much happier.

"That's great. I'm happy for you!" I said.

"I also quit the soccer team," she confessed.

"I'm sorry. I know you tried really hard."

"I'm better off. I hated it."

After we finished dinner, we went searching for shelter. Since I was only nineteen at the time, there weren't too many places to book a room. After twenty minutes of driving through town, I found this motel off the beaten path. Most of the lights were out on the sign, and it reminded me of the motel in the movie 'Psycho.' It had a creepy look to it, and there were prostitutes scattered all over the trash filled parking lot.

This looks like a great placed to be stabbed...with syphilis.

I went up to the window of the front office. It was covered in cobwebs, and I could barely see inside. There was a paper-thin Indian man standing in the main office with glasses.

"Yes. Can I get a room for two nights please?" I asked.

"Yes, buddy. No problem. $29.95," the man said.

Does that include champagne and a heart shaped hot tub?

I opened the door to our room, which made a loud creaking sound like it was a thousand years old. Inside were two queen beds, a flickering lamp, and a TV from the year I was born. The room smelled like burnt cigarettes, but it was better than sleeping in my car.

Or was it?

Once we got settled in, our hormones began to come back to life. Neither one of us had been sexually active in awhile. I guess it was time to dust off our private parts and get it on. We fell into the bed while kissing. The mattress was as hard as a rock, but we began to intertwine nonetheless. We undressed each other rapidly, and I was about to breach the vaginal entrance. All of a sudden, Jayden stopped me.

"Wait. Do you have a condom?" she asked.

"No. Aren't you on birth control?" I said.

"No. I stopped."

DAMMIT!

"Go get some, and come back quick," she said.

There I was, hard as a rock, about to walk outside where hookers hunt boners like starving sharks.

I got in my car and drove to the nearest gas station. I walked inside and ran over to the isle with the condoms. I grabbed a box, and bolted to the counter.

"I just need to buy these as fast as I can," I said.

"Um. Ok. Something about to go down?" the attendant replied.

"Yes. There's no time!"

"Here you go, my brotha. Good luck."

I drove back as fast as I could, but I was losing the power inside my pants. I pulled up to the motel hoping that I wouldn't see any crime scene tape wrapped around our door. This place was shady as fuck, and I'm fairly certain that someone would be murdered there that evening.

I busted the door open, strapped on my hard hat, and got to work. It was an awkward moment for both of us because we hadn't engaged in sex for eight months. While I was attempting to sexually maneuver my way in and out, something strange happened.

A powerful gust of wind shot out, which vibrated the entire bed frame. I didn't know if it had come from me…or her.

"What the hell was that?" I asked.

We both stared at each other with confusion and neither one of us knew what to say. We went about our business although I'm pretty sure one of us was just 'dutch-ovened.'

After about ten minutes, we called it a night. The romance just wasn't there like before. The sexual fire that was burning inside us back in high school…had been extinguished.

The remainder of the weekend, I started to question the integrity of the relationship. I wasn't exactly happy with the way things were going. I was afraid that if I were honest with Jayden about what I felt, her life would shatter once again. I didn't know if I should continue down this mysterious path. I marched on blinded by my naïve nature.

Throughout the remainder of the spring semester, I made only a couple more trips to see Jayden. Money was tight, the gas prices were going up, and the crime rate was rising at our shitty motel.

Jayden decided to move home for the summer to be close to her parents. I was working a lot to save money and when I had time, I would often visit Jayden at her parent's house. It was like we had been sucked back into the past; like we were back in high school again, but this time, the atmosphere was much different.

Every time I went to her house, there was tension that was climbing all over the walls. Her parents would give me odd looks all the time as if I was a criminal. It felt like I was always walking on a tight rope throughout their house about to be pushed to my death.

Unexpectedly, in the middle of the summer break, Jayden transferred to the same college I was at. I was not exactly ready for this, but I guess it made sense. She got an apartment off campus down the street from where I was. School began shortly after Jayden got settled in.

By having Jayden close by, the old feelings that I had buried were rising up to the surface. I didn't know if these feelings were coming back because I was falling in love again or because they were leftovers from a previous life. It was like I had just accepted the fact that this was the woman I was going to be with. I was forcing the feelings through to make it work, like a plunger on a clogged toilet.

We were still sexually active, but it was becoming more and more uneventful. I knew I was partly to blame, but the sex was objective, not sentimental. We did it to feel like a normal couple. We embraced only the missionary position and very rarely experimented with any foreplay. Sometimes Jayden would start to cry right in the middle of sex for unknown reasons. It was very bizarre and extremely awkward.

"Do you want me to stop?" I asked.

"No, just keep going. Just ignore my tears," she replied.

Jesus, this is fucking awful.

As the months went by, I felt like I was once again forcing the relationship to work just like I did in the final moments of our first love story. School kept us both pretty busy, but everyday was a battle trying NOT to break up. I was worn thin, trying to do everything I could to make her happy. I slowly began to realize that I was doing these things out of pity and not out of love. My body ached, my mind was fatigued, and my libido was curled up in the corner crying itself to sleep every night.

Without warning, Jayden began to morph into an apathetic type of creature. She became distant, evasive, and non-affectionate. She had powered down so to speak. It was like the old Jayden from high school had appeared once again. Soon thereafter, she began to make mysterious trips back to her old college town for weekend get-a-ways.

"I'm just going up there to see some of my good girlfriends," she would tell me.

During these excursions, she would never call or text me, which was strange. I knew something was fishy. Who knew what scandalous things were happening up there? We hadn't connected sexually in two months, and she was most likely getting nailed by someone else.

There was adultery afoot, and I could sense it.

One day, Jayden arrived at my apartment from one of her 'sperm-blasting' vacations. The culpable look on her face was unmistakable. I could immediately tell that something was wrong by her lack of emotion towards me. She went to the bathroom, most likely to purge her stomach or relieve herself of any foreign toxins. She had left her purse in my room. I went to take a short glance at her phone to see if I could find any incriminating texts or calls. As I looked inside, I noticed two unopened condom packets. They were the spermicidal rubbers by Trojan, which I had never purchased in my life.

Jayden walked out of the bathroom and came into my room. I had the condoms sitting on my desk. She looked at me with a blank stare.

I yelled, "I'm so glad that you are protecting yourself when you're having sex with SOMEBODY ELSE!"

"I can explain," she said.

"Since you blessed me with two condoms, I will in turn give you two chances to explain to me why the hell you have these in your purse."

"Juddy, those have been in there forever. We just never used them."

"You're God damn right, because I have never bought these before. Let's try this again."

"Ok. I have been seeing someone else for the past few weeks."

"No shit."

"I wanted to tell you, but I knew you would get mad."

"Ha-Ha! Get the fuck out of my apartment."

Jayden quickly grabbed all of her things and blazed, slamming the door on her way out.

Two weeks later, Jayden was already in a relationship with the guy she had been boning behind my back. She had enlisted my services to reestablish her perfect image with her parents. Once that was done, my job was over. I was attempting to help her, but instead I came out looking like an imbecile.

I was torn apart once again, and I was having trouble dealing with my depressive reality. My world became filled with anger, and I wanted to know why this was happening to me. I didn't deserve this bullshit, and I was emotionally worn thin.

With the seed of depression planted inside me, I knew I had to stop it from growing. Even though my dishonesty may have caused this relationship to fail, I was still drenched in sadness. I didn't know where to turn. I didn't know who to talk to.

This was only the beginning of the long dark road of busted love stories.

Relationship Report:

Pros	Cons
• Athletic Build	• Short Term Alcoholic
• Intelligent	• Cheater
• Nice Teeth	• Apathetic
• High School Sweetheart	• Blame-Shifter
• Road Head Compatible	• Birth Control Activist

Total Time Lost	4 years, 5 months
Hours of Unpaid Labor	200
Cheated?	Yes
Emotional Trauma (On a Scale of 1 to 10)	7
Sex Life	Average
Physical Abuse	No

Total Montary Loses:
$21,995.00

- Dinner Dates: 4x per month @ $60 per date
- Special Occasion Dates: 1x every 6 months @ $150.00 per date
- Gifts (Holidays and Anniversaries): 6x per year @ $100.00 per gift
- Commuting Gas Consumption: $1,200 per year.

Chapter 4-Ravenna: 'The Cocaine Tree Giant' Part 1

After about four months of focusing on school, I was feeling somewhat normal again. There was still some scar tissue left over from the previous relationship. I didn't want my negative past to affect my future. I was ready to get back out there, and start fresh again.

The beginning of a new semester was always a good time in college because a new crop of women would magically appear. Once school started, the sororities hosted an event called 'Bid Day.' It was a recruitment event that involved the selection of specific girls to seven different sororities. It was the largest gathering of women on campus during the school year and also the largest gathering of hungry frat boys.

Bid Day took place at the sorority houses, which were big white dormitories scattered on a grassy hill of non-stop drama and empty wine bottles.

The event was filled with gorgeous women frolicking all over the place. We were like a pack of wolves waiting to get a taste of the female flesh. There was one girl who stood above the rest. She looked like a blonde oak tree. She was six feet tall, and compared to her, the other girls looked like peasants.

This towering woman must have come from another planet.

She had long legs and dark tan skin. Her platinum blonde hair blinded my eyes, and she was quite intimidating. I was thinking of ways to approach this sorority row giant, but of course, I had to do recon before I climbed the beanstalk. I began to ask girls, who were friends of mine in her sorority, about her.

Her name was Ravenna. She was an education major and fairly active in the sorority. Currently, she was not dating anyone. There was nothing that raised any red flags, but I didn't have a smooth way to approach her. I took my time until an opportunity arose.

My fraternity had elected me to the social chairman position that year. My job duties were to basically throw parties throughout the semester without letting anyone get arrested or killed. The position gave me an opportunity to get to know a lot of the sorority girls around campus. It was the dream job of our fraternity, but it also came with much responsibility.

One particular night, we had a social gathering with Ravenna's sorority at a local club we had rented out. It was a small venue with a dance floor, six bartenders, and a DJ. The theme for the party was 'Cowboys and Indians.'

I decided to go as an Indian.

I had red tribal paint on my face, a headband with a feather, and a pair of moccasins. Once I arrived at the party I was anxiously waiting for Ravenna to show up. I tipped back about three shots of vodka to increase my confidence level.

Ravenna arrived with her sorority a few minutes later. She had on brown Ugg boots, a short brown skirt, and a small piece of cloth that was hanging on for dear life around her chest. She looked like Pocahontas, if Pocahontas she was a stripper. I had to pick my jaw off the floor as I awkwardly gazed while she was dancing.

Luckily, a fraternity brother of mine named Jack was dating Ravenna's roommate. He introduced us, and we began to get to know each other.

I told Ravenna, "I hope you don't mind that I'm shorter than you. Your height was the first thing that I was attracted to."

She replied, "Well thank you. Most men are afraid of me but I really am a nice girl."

We hung out the entire night, dancing and drinking the whole way. She was energetic, friendly, and very pretty. While we were on the dance floor, I happened to notice that Ravenna also had a particular anatomical feature that was glowing like the moon. She had an exquisite gluteus maximus. It was round, supple, and you could even set your drink on top of it for convenience.

Towards the end of the night the last call for alcohol came. This was always the very last chance for the guys to seal the deal with a female counterpart. Naturally, every guy in the place rushed to the bar like a pack of hungry hyenas. We were all attempting to purchase one final drink. I ordered Ravenna an apple martini. It was a drink with class and a hint of cough syrup.

After we finished our final round of drinks Ravenna and her roommate invited Jack and me over to hang out at the sorority house. I rode with Jack while Ravenna and her roommate took her car back home.

Halfway back, a very powerful force hit my intestinal area. I almost blacked out, and there was no turning back. I had to release the demon inside me at the absolute nearest disposal facility.

I looked Jack square in the eyes and said, "Dude, there is something horrible happening inside me right now. I need you to take me to the closest gas station before I spontaneously combust."

"No problem, dude. Are you going to be ok?" Jack asked.

"It is too early to tell," I replied as sweat began to fall down my forehead.

"Shit."

I had a gigantic fear of using public restrooms, but this was my only chance with Ravenna and I couldn't blow it. Just like how I was about to blow the lid off an innocent toilet in about ten seconds.

Jack quickly pulled into the gas station parking lot. I leapt from the vehicle while it was still moving and ran as fast as I could. Suddenly, everything seemed like it was in slow motion. Once I busted through the front door, I ran past a small child looking at candy. I palmed his tiny head like a basketball and shoved him out of the way.

The child screamed in annoyance.

I yelled, "THERE'S NO TIME, SON!"

I finally reached the bathroom after what felt like a 100-meter dash. What actually transpired inside that dark place I will never speak of again. There was nothing but pure evil that came out of me.

After the catastrophic bowel movement in that desolate lavatory, I felt like I had just gone through a colonoscopy. I walked out of the bathroom, apologized to the child I pushed over and got back into Jack's car. I immediately realized that we needed a story to tell the girls to cover up the crime that I had just committed.

I frantically said to Jack, "If Ravenna knows that I stopped to drop a load off, she will never speak to me again."

We arrived at the sorority house, and I was lighter on my feet than usual. We entered through the back door and walked upstairs.

Once we walked into Ravenna's room, both of the girls asked us what took so long.

We quickly made up a story of how we went to Taco Bell to get some food, and there was a long drive-thru line we had to wait in. The irony of it all was that Taco Bell was most likely the cause of the porcelain explosion that just happened.

They both gave us befuddled looks, and I was worried that the mission was compromised.

We went about our business, and all four of us conversed for a while in the tiny dorm room. We then decided to put on a movie. About fifteen minutes later, I was swapping spit with Ravenna on her black futon, which had a low quality cushion that felt like cardboard. I didn't want her to think I was too aggressive and was only there to bang. I had to play it cool, so I decided to remain in the preliminary kissing stage.

I ended up spending the night which was illegal in the sorority code.

I like to live dangerously…what can I say?

After we woke up, Ravenna said, "I had a great time with you, but you must be careful on your way out."

I asked, "What will they do if they see me?"

"They might put me on social probation or fine me."

"As long as I don't get in trouble, I'm good."

Ravenna started to laugh.

I quietly walked out of the room. My head was pounding, and I was still drunk. I also still had my Indian clothes on from the night before. I tiptoed down the hallway but my balance was completely off.

I looked like a fucking moron.

After I reached the bottom floor of the house, I proceeded to the front door. I then heard some snickering and laughter behind me. I turned around and sitting at a large round table was the entire pledge class along with the president of the sorority.

Stephanie, the president, said, "What in the hell are you doing?"

I said, "Trying to find Pocahontas."

All the girls began to laugh including Stephanie.

She casually yelled, "Get out of here before our advisor gets here!"

I ran out the front door as quickly as I could, making Indian calls with my hands and mouth the whole way.

Like I said. I was still drunk.

Ravenna and I had exchanged numbers the night before. We texted back and forth quite a bit the following days after the sorority slumber party. I didn't know if I was truly ready to get involved in another relationship just yet, but I decided to pursue the colossal woman.

In preparation for our first date, I took two multi-symptom Imodium pills. I wasn't about to let my stomach dictate the success of our very first date. I drove to go pick her up at the sorority house. As she walked through the back door I couldn't take my eyes off her. She was wearing jeans that were grasping her buttocks tightly and a red blouse with heels. She had a smile on her face and I was excited.

"Hey, Juddy. Thanks for picking me up. Sorry for the audience," she said.

"Audience?" I asked in confusion.

I then looked up at the second story of the sorority house. There were girls lined up against every window awkwardly staring at us. It was as if Ravenna was leaving the sorority orphanage to start a new life, and they were saying goodbye.

"So how was your day? I had a stressful day! I'm ready for a drink!" she said in exhaustion.

"Me too!" I anxiously replied.

I'm always ready for a drink.

I took us to a nearby Mexican food place. It was half-off fajita Tuesday, so I was in luck. Once we sat down, we wasted no time in getting hammered. We ordered two large margaritas with a Corona beer stuck upside down in the top of it. It looked like an alcoholic flagpole stuck in the sand. It was known as a 'beer-rita,' and they were absolutely delicious.

During our dinner conversation, Ravenna told me that she was quite impressed with my manners. She said that her past boyfriends had all been complete dicks. Most of them had cheated on her and treated her like shit.

I told her, "I'm sorry for what you have been through. They had no right to treat you that way."

Ravenna admitted, "Sometimes I feel like I just always meet the wrong guys."

After dinner, we went back to my apartment and picked out a movie to watch. We decided on 'Forgetting Sarah Marshall,' which ironically, was a movie about a terrible break-up.

I prayed to God that this flick was not a foreshadowing of what's to come.

While we were on the couch, I decided to go in for a kiss. Ravenna gracefully accepted. While we were making out, she grabbed my hand and slowly guided it towards her southern hemisphere, which was quite warm this time of year.

I was a little surprised that she shoved my hand into her underworld so quickly. We then began to violently strip each other's clothes off.

We were butt-naked pretty quick, which led to an all-out anatomical excursion. I was forced into foreplay positions that I never knew existed. Something told me she was more experienced in this line of work than I was. We didn't have sex, but we came extremely close to the edge of intercourse.

I had to catch my breath once it was all over.

Ravenna said, "I'm sorry. I get pretty aggressive when it comes to tequila."

I replied, "Really? I couldn't tell."

While watching the remainder of the movie, we passed out on the couch. Since she was the taller human, I had to accept the little spoon position. She had me wrapped up tight like a mama bear keeping her cub warm.

It was a damn good night, mainly due to the effective ingredients of Imodium…and tequila.

During the first few weeks we were together, I was trying to get to know her on a more emotional level. I wanted to decipher her intentions without seeming too intrusive. My guard was definitely up, and I was worried about getting fucked over again. Any weak links in the old ball and chain could be very dangerous. Nothing seemed abnormal, and we were getting along fairly well.

We were both social people, so we enjoyed going out a lot. We would attend many house parties together and go to every bar in town about three times a week. I don't know how the hell I went days on end drinking nonstop. My body back then could bounce back from a hangover automatically with any hesitation.

Nowadays, I end up in an alcohol induced coma if I have more than two cocktails. Getting old sucks.

Everything seemed to be going as planned. I made sure I was taking care of her as best I could. I had been raised as a people pleaser by my parents, and I always enjoyed being kind to others.

Seeing Ravenna happy…made me happy.

Toward the end of each semester, Ravenna's sorority held a 'prom-style' event called Formal. This event was awesome mainly due to the fact that it was the one time where the woman paid for everything. Every sorority member had the responsibility of making their Formal date a gift basket filled with their favorite liquor and snacks. The girls also pitched in for a large banquet hall, a formal dinner, and a chartered bus ride to and from the event.

I wish these types of events still existed in the post-college world.

Everyone met at the sorority house to load up for the trip. Ravenna wore a long black dress with diamonds scattered at the top of it. She had her blonde hair curled and her skin was radiant, which was due to an accurately applied spray tan. She had on tall silver heels and towered over me, but it was completely worth it. Ravenna was the sky-high Greek queen of the night, and I was honored to be her date.

We hopped inside the bus and pulled out our premade fruit punch vodka bomb. We began to drink…heavily. When we arrived at the country club, we were guided to the banquet hall. None of us could walk straight and about half of the attendees were already piss drunk.

Inside the large ballroom, there were chandeliers, ice sculptures, and multiple tables that were lined with sterling silver utensils. There was a big wooden dance floor in the middle and an outdoor balcony with a mountain of champagne bottles stacked on the side of it.

Time to get wasted and dance like an idiot.

Ravenna and I had a great time together at Formal. We danced all night long, had an amazing four-course meal, and consumed a large amount of alcohol. Inevitably, by the end of the night, we were both shitfaced.

After it was over, all the drunks at the party loaded up onto the bus like a bunch of slow moving zombies. There were a few guests who were blowing chunks along the way. Thankfully, we were not among them.

On the ride back, we decided to resume our binge drinking. My canteen of vodka was empty, so I grabbed the closest alcoholic beverage next to me. It was a wine bag that had been plucked out of its Franzia box. I propped it on top of my shoulder like it was an I.V. bag. I opened the spout at the bottom to feed Ravenna and I some White Zinfandel. It was like we were in the Sahara desert, and these were the last few drops of water.

After draining the entire bag, we started to viciously make out. We were tongue twisted for the majority of the ride back. There were others on the bus that decided to go far beyond kissing, and that made me slightly uncomfortable. There was even a couple having sex in the bathroom of the bus, which was about the same size as one on an airplane.

Stay classy partygoers.

Once we got back on campus, everyone drunkenly funneled out of the bus. It looked like the bus was a dump truck unloading dead bodies onto the pavement. Luckily, my apartment complex was walking distance from where we were dropped off. Ravenna took off her heels, and we made our way up to my building. The hike up to the third story was tough mainly because I was gazing at Ravenna's butt cheeks moving left to right with every step she took. I opened the front door, took her by the hand, and guided her to where the magic was about to happen.

Both of us were hammered and horny.

Once we got in my room, we quickly undressed each other. Before I made the vaginal voyage, I reached over to my dresser and grabbed a trusty love glove. All of a sudden, Ravenna stopped me and said, "Don't worry about that. I've been on birth control for years."

The sound of Enya's voice from 'Lord of the Rings' entered my ears. It was as if a bright light had shined upon me and bestowed a warm blanket of happiness over my soul. I had never embarked on a journey like this without a protective shield. Without hesitation, I took the plunge into the unknown.

The sensation overall was quite impressive. It was a night and day difference. I had to make sure I concentrated on going the distance and making the encounter last. I tried to think of things that would enhance my intercourse longevity. I thought of clowns, cold showers, and even dead kittens. Anything that would distract my mind from the volcano that was about to erupt.

Then, about twenty minutes later, the time had come. The eject button had been pressed. As soon as the escape plan was executed, there was only a short amount of time to determine the landing zone of the baby producing liquid. Any hesitation on my part could absolutely cause death…or life.

God, I hope she wasn't lying about being on the pill.

Before I was able to calculate the coordinates, the projectile launched with great velocity. The scud missile flew through the air and right into Ravenna's left nasal cavity.

"Are you fucking serious?" Ravenna exclaimed in anger.

"Holy shit! I'm so sorry," I said.

"I think I'm going to throw up."

Ravenna began to gag and cough at the same time.

Here we go again.

She ran over to the sink, plugged up her right nostril with her finger, and let the spermicidal snot rocket fly.

Ravenna yelled, "If you ever do that again, I'll kill you."

"Well I wasn't intentionally trying to do it. You have to admit though; that was impeccable aiming," I said.

I guess some protective glasses wouldn't be such a bad idea in the future. The last thing I wanted to do was cripple her with blindness. That would be a great story for our illegitimate children.

It had been six months with Ravenna, and our relationship was moving to a more serious role. We were spending a lot of time together and we were happy. I hadn't yet made the big step of meeting her parents, but I knew it was coming. If they could see what type of man I was, they would certainly realize that I would treat their daughter with respect. The ultimate battle would be the approval of the Father. It could go very well or completely backfire.

Sure enough one day Ravenna asked me, "Would you like to go to my cousin's wedding with me as my date?"

I would be meeting her entire Father's side of the family all at once. At first, I felt a little overwhelmed, but I knew I had to do this in order to provide a solid foundation for the future of our relationship. Ravenna said that if I felt uncomfortable about it I didn't have to go. I never hesitated once in accepting the invitation because it wasn't about me. I was doing it for her.

I said in excitement, "Absolutely! I would be honored."

A few weeks later, Ravenna and I drove about two hours outside town to the wedding. It was held at this old white mansion on a large piece of land out in the country. One of the first things we did when we arrived was meet up with her parents before the ceremony began.

It was time to put on my game face. I was trying to be confident but not cocky. First impressions are key, and I wanted to make sure I didn't screw it up.

As we walked up to the seating area Ravenna said, "My parents are over there on the right."

They were just as tall as Ravenna. I looked like a small hobbit about to introduce myself to a couple of tree giants. I made sure my voice was deeper than usual to provide a sense of manliness.

Ravenna said, "Mom, Dad. This is Juddy, my boyfriend."

"Nice to meet you, Juddy. I'm, David and this is, Alison."

"Pleased to meet you, Mr. and Mrs. Thompson," I replied.

We all took our seats and the ceremony began. As the groom stood at the altar, I could see the sweat seeping from his forehead. This was a very big day for him. Even I was nervous for the poor bastard. He was about to take the big plunge.

One day, hopefully, I would be in his shoes. I actually looked forward to getting married. It was too early to tell if Ravenna was the one.

The bride then rode up to the altar in a white carriage with two Clydesdale horses.

I hope these massive animals don't take a massive shit during the reading of the vows.

After the ceremony, Ravenna and her mother headed inside to use the restroom. It was just her father and I at the table. There was a brief moment of silence. I was trying to come up with some sort of icebreaker but coming up with nothing.

Then her father asked, "So how did you and Ravenna meet?"

I replied, "We met through one of my fraternity's social events."

If her father only knew what Ravenna was wearing the night of the 'Cowboys and Indians' he would shit himself.

One question led to another, and we began to delve into a serious man-to-man talk.

Her father had a large amount of displeasure towards the ex-boyfriends of his only daughter.

In a stern voice he said, "They were all terrible guys and one of them was even a drug dealer."

I could see the anger in his eyes. I felt that anyone who would cross paths with him would probably not survive. A small amount of fear ran down my spine thinking of what those large fists would do to my face.

I told him, "I have been raised in a home where women are treated with respect and I assure you that I intend to do everything in my power to make your daughter happy. She is very special to me."

He replied, "It looks like Ravenna has finally for once made a wise decision. She has been known to make poor choices."

I started to get the notion that her father had more anger towards Ravenna rather than her ex-boyfriends. Maybe Ravenna was one of those girls that enjoyed dating assholes.

I will never understand that ridiculous mentality.

If that were true, then obviously she was with the wrong guy.

Finally, Ravenna and her mother came back and we all got in the buffet line to eat. The rest of the wedding was pretty relaxed. We danced to a few good songs, and I was introduced to most of Ravenna's family members. They were all very nice and overall, it was a great night for the both of us.

A few weeks later, Ravenna enrolled in summer school while I stayed busy with my part time job. Since Ravenna only needed an apartment for the summer months, she found one of the cheapest places on campus.

It was an old, musty wooden complex located on the outskirts of town. The apartment was very small and had a certain stench that smelled like a damp towel. Ravenna didn't even have a real bed. She had a twin-sized futon, which was not exactly ideal for two adults to sleep on. The appliances in the kitchen were outdated by at least two decades. The carpet had numerous stains as if there had been multiple homicides inside. There was absolutely nothing appealing about this place…except the price.

While habitating in that stale desolate apartment, I found that our moods were changing. The quality of our living quarters was affecting our relationship. She was stressed at school, and I was burnt-out at work. We would always be so tired when we got home that our intimacy began to fizzle away. I knew that soon the dark dwelling would consume us like a haunted house.

I began to think of things I could do for Ravenna to help us deal with the emotional rut we were in. Surely by performing good deeds, we would be in a better state of mind.

Ravenna's car was always a complete mess on the inside. She would always claim she never had time to clean it. At first glance, it literally looked like she was living out of it. There was always a strange lingering odor coming from the back seat. I honestly didn't know how she drove around without becoming nauseated. It was like Ravenna had adapted to the smell and just accepted it as a part of her life. I don't know where it came from, but it was agitating me. I had to put a stop to it before something inside the car sprouted legs and tried to kill her.

One day, I woke up early while Ravenna was still sleeping and took her keys. I drove her car to the nearest detail center. I went up to the clerk and said, "I need this car completely detailed. Your technician may need to wear a mask and gloves."

That poor bastard worked on her car for three hours, while I went and had breakfast next door. Finally, the car was spotless and the strange odor had disappeared. I drove the car back to Ravenna's apartment. She was awake by then, and when I walked in the door she asked, "Where have you been?"

I said, "I just saved your life and the life of your vehicle."

I guided her outside to her bright white four-door sedan. She couldn't believe her eyes.

"Thank you so much for doing that! It looks brand new! I know it's been quite a mess in there for awhile," she said.

That night we decided to take her spotless car out for a fresh joy ride. We went to a local watering hole to have drinks. Ravenna had just wrapped up all of her finals for summer school, and it was time to get wasted. We chose a drink that packed a punch. It was filled with tears, anger, and regret.

"Two Jaeger-Bombs, please!" I yelled.

Let the binge drinking begin.

Ravenna was guzzling alcohol like it was going out of style. I was trying to keep up but she was kicking my ass. We stayed there until the entire bar shut down for the night. Ravenna was stumbling on her way out. I used all the strength I had to throw her lifeless body into the car like a dead hooker.

We then headed back to her apartment. As soon as we pulled into the parking lot, Ravenna stopped me from getting out of the car by grasping my belt buckle. She jerked me back into the car like I was a rag doll. Once I was back inside the vehicle, she grabbed my shirt and pulled me close.

In a deep satanic voice she said, "Let's get in the back seat and FUCK!"

It seemed that the Jaeger had fueled the sexual beast inside, and she was ready to decimate my body. I immediately realized that this escapade would test the flexibility of our bodies. I reluctantly squeezed into the back seat.

This could quite possibly be the most uncomfortable sex ever, but hey, I'm not complaining.

While we were making out her voice became deeper and more evil.

Ravenna growled, "LEAVE YOUR CLOTHES ON AND JUST GET INSIDE ME!"

I started to shake in fear and I knew I didn't have a choice.

Having sex with your clothes on is like eating a banana without peeling it. It's much more enjoyable when you strip the outer layer off.

While the back-seat sex was underway, the integrity of the vehicle's suspension springs was revealed. Not only was the car moving in a seesaw type of motion, but the screeching high-pitched sound of the springs echoed through the parking lot. Furthermore, Ravenna's vehicle had no tint of any kind. Even with the fogged up windows, anyone could see right through.

I decided to see if there were any peeping toms about the premises. I happened to glance over at a truck that was parked three spaces over from us. Inside the truck was an old fellow reading a newspaper. This was quite strange because it was three in the morning. I guess he just enjoyed catching up on current events inside his car during the early waking hours.

All of a sudden, the old man turned and looked right at me. I immediately froze as if I had seen a ghost. He was catching me in one of the most vulnerable moments of my life. I was completely defenseless with my wiener nestled inside Ravenna.

I had never locked eyes with a male during intercourse. It was completely awkward in so many ways. It was like he was in the car with us.

Ravenna exclaimed, "What the hell are you looking at? Look at me! Not the fucking window!"

The old man then calmly tipped his hat to me as a sign of respect for getting laid that night. He went back to reading his newspaper, but after that moment, my sexual drive immediately began to shutdown.

Ravenna asked, "What's wrong?"

I said, "Can we go inside and finish the job in a more secluded area?"

We went inside and tried to salvage any remaining stiffness. Afterwards, we both slipped into a Jaeger-induced sleep.

Well that's just great. I just spent money detailing her car and we just defiled the shit out of it.

Our relationship became much better after Ravenna moved out of those shitty apartments. Our moods were better, and we were growing stronger as a couple. Our one-year anniversary was coming up, and I wanted to do something special for her. Luckily, my parents had plans to go out of town soon.

Sound familiar?

My parents had a Jacuzzi and I figured it would be great to get in the hot tub, share some drinks, and have a romantic evening together.

I wanted to be top shelf that night, but I was on a budget. I went to the one place where dreams die.

Wal-Mart.

I bought three bottles of cheap champagne and a dozen roses. I also ordered Chinese takeout which was our favorite.

Before Ravenna arrived, I made sure I had everything ready. I cranked up the Jacuzzi to 100 degrees, put the bottles of champagne on ice, and set the table.

There was a knock at the door, and I could see the silhouette of a tall being through the front glass pane. My heart began to race. I opened the door, and my beautiful giant had arrived

"Welcome, my love! Here's to a night of fried rice, champagne, and passion!" I said.

She chuckled, "Thank you so much for doing this. No one has ever done anything like this for me before."

"It's been a wonderful year together!"

We both sat down at the dinner table where I had neatly organized the lovely meal of shrimp fried rice, won ton soup, and orange chicken. I didn't cook the food, but I presented it with lavish grace.

The steam coming off the rice was a breath of fresh air. I opened the first bottle of champagne and poured us two glasses. It didn't take us too long to devour our Chinese cuisine.

After dinner, we both went to go change into our bathing suits. I walked out of the bathroom and Ravenna was standing in the hallway with a lime green bikini.

"You look amazing in that two-piece," I said.

"Oh, shut up," Ravenna chuckled.

We walked outside to submerge our skin in the steaming hot Jacuzzi. I brought the bottles of champagne, which I then neatly placed on a bed of ice inside my cooler.

Ravenna and I finished all the champagne pretty quickly. We were swimming in a small ocean of alcohol. We began to lock lips and enjoy the moment together. Our hands also began to migrate in and around each other's bathing suits. The night was going extremely well…so far.

Then all of a sudden, Ravenna said to me in a shaky voice, "Juddy, there is something that I need to tell you, and it's quite embarrassing."

Shit. What now?

I replied, "Don't ever be afraid to tell me something. We need to be open and honest with each other."

She then began to reveal to me a story that would change my perception of her…forever.

Chapter 5-Ravenna: 'The Cocaine Tree Giant' Part 2

In the not too distant past, during the first few weeks we were dating, Ravenna had been using cocaine on a regular basis. She used it a lot while she worked at a sports bar to stay awake during long shifts.

"It was the only way I could stay awake," she explained.

Apparently, she was unaware of the all-natural legal stimulatory drink called coffee.

One night after she got off from her shift around 2am, she went and had drinks with some of her coworkers. She also decided to indulge in some blow. Ravenna then left her friend's house and headed home, which was an hour away.

Halfway home, while on the freeway, Ravenna lost control of her car. She smashed right into the middle cement barrier that divided southbound and northbound traffic. The hood of the car was smashed in all the way to the windshield.

She was luckily in one piece with no injuries, and there were no other vehicles involved. The police quickly arrived at the scene and began to search the inside of her car. The police didn't find anything incriminating, but unbeknownst to the officers, there was a bag of cocaine hidden underneath the driver's seat.

They began to perform field sobriety tests on Ravenna. Inevitably, she failed each and every test. Ravenna was charged with driving while intoxicated, speeding, and failure to maintain her lane. She was taken to jail that evening and bailed out by her parents the next morning.

Ravenna's parents spent over $20,000 in legal fees to get the charges erased from her record forever. This process took several months. The gravity of these criminal charges would have destroyed any chances of a career in teaching, which was what she wanted to do after she graduated. Ravenna was quite upset during the unraveling of this story, and she began to cry.

"I just want to be honest with you that's all. I know you must hate me now," she sobbed.

"I don't hate you. I just don't understand why you never told me this," I replied.

"I was afraid that you would leave me."

"Thank you for being honest with me, but I have to ask. Are still using?"

"No. Not anymore."

The problem for me was that this incident took place right under my nose, and I had no idea. Doubt began to cloud my mind. I was worried that there might be other dark secrets that Ravenna was hiding from me.

I didn't want to feel this way again. The last time I did, my trust was annihilated.

I told her, "Ravenna, we have to be honest with each other. I may find it hard to completely trust you right now, but I know that you never wanted to hurt me."

"I'm so sorry for not telling you. I will never do that again. I love you," she said.

I'm so glad she decided to spill her guts on this joyous occasion.

After that night, I began to question our relationship. The seed of doubt had been planted. I was confused but at the same time, everyone makes mistakes. Maybe she was in a bad place and needed help turning her life around. I was willing to sacrifice my distrust in her in order to make her happy. I knew I loved her, but I was very apprehensive of the future. I was taking a risk in continuing the relationship, but I didn't want to give up on her.

A few weeks later, we were invited to go have dinner with Ravenna's friend and her husband. We went to a nice Italian place on the river walk. All four of us sat down and began to examine the menu. Our guests were very nice, and we all were getting along.

After we ordered our food, Ravenna's phone began to go off. There were multiple text messages and calls that were flooding her cell phone. She finally put the phone on silent, but there was an awkward feeling at the dinner table. Ravenna looked at me with a nervous twitch and it was incredibly unnerving.

Midway through dinner, Ravenna got up to use the restroom.

She said, "Will you excuse me? My father has been calling me. I'm just going to go call him back real quick."

She was in the bathroom for about ten minutes. She was either on the phone the entire time or taking a big dump. Ravenna had a distressed look on her face when she came back to the table.

I asked, "Is everything ok?"

Ravenna reluctantly replied, "Yeah, everything is fine."

I felt that she was lying to me. I didn't want to cause a scene at dinner, so I kept my composure. All four of us at the table went on with our dinner. We shared a few laughs, and then went our separate ways. On the ride home, Ravenna was real quiet, which was unusual.

I asked, "Are you alright? You have been silent the entire car ride."

She replied, "Yeah, I'm just tired, that's all."

I started to feel stressed. I didn't know what was going through her head, and I was praying that she wasn't lying to me about the phone call.

We got home and put on a movie. She didn't say too much, and afterwards, we headed to bed. I never confronted her about it again. I didn't want to accuse her, but at the same time I felt like I had a right to know the truth.

Her behavior began change after that night. She was distant at times, but I figured she maybe needed space. The mystery of the phone call was eating away at me, but I didn't want to cause any turmoil between us. I kept my feelings inside about it and moved on.

Ravenna's sorority had a date party coming up. There were about a hundred of us attending. The theme of the party was 'Revenge of the Nerds.' It was probably one of my favorite party themes in college. My costume included suspenders, a bowtie, high water pants, and dorky glasses. I was basically the white version of Urkel.

Ravenna had on a plaid skirt, white button down shirt, and double ponytails.

The sorority had not only rented out a large school bus for the trip, they also reserved the bar we were heading to for the night. It was a two-story Irish pub outside of town.

That night, of the event all the attendees piled into the school bus carrying an assortment of liquor and beer. The guys also came prepared with large empty Gatorade jugs to relieve themselves on the forty-five minute journey. Sometimes these urine filled jugs were disposed of out the window.

Lord only knows how many cars we pelted with high-speed piss.

Ravenna and I sat towards the back of the bus on the ride there. During the ride, she kept on asking me about my buddy Brian, who was on the bus with us.

"Is he dating anyone? He's cute," she asked.

"I have no idea," I mumbled.

"I want to hook him up with one of my girlfriends."

"This is a date party, so I am guessing he has a date tonight."

"Yeah I know."

I was not against Ravenna playing matchmaker. It was just odd to me that she decided to ask me that question knowing it would make me feel insecure. Although, I didn't want her to know that I was uncomfortable, I was afraid of looking weak.

When we arrived at the bar, Ravenna began to ignore me. She began to talk to Brian and his date during the party.

I've seen this type of behavior before from someone else.

Occasionally, Ravenna would acknowledge my presence, but all in all, it was insulting. I just hung out with my buddies and got wasted. Some of the guys even asked me, "Where is Ravenna? I haven't seen you with her all night."

On the way home, Ravenna and I sat in the same spot towards the back of the bus. She invited Brian and his date to sit near us. Ravenna and Brian began to converse with each other. The bus had no air conditioning, so it was pretty hot inside. Brian took off his button down shirt and had a tank top underneath. He was a pretty ripped dude, and Ravenna really couldn't take her eyes off of him.

She then asked, "Brian, do you work out?"

Give me a fucking break.

Brian didn't hear her ask the question. It was quite loud inside the bus of drunks.

He eventually began to make out with his date, which was what I thought I would be doing with Ravenna. I felt so humiliated by the fact that she ignored me. I had been her boyfriend for over a year, and the only thing that night turned into…was a slap in the face.

When we got back to campus, I told Ravenna I wasn't feeling well, and that I just wanted to go home by myself to rest.

"Ok. No problem," she said.

She didn't even try to see if there was anything she could do for me. I took a long walk back to my apartment feeling a sense of rejection. The college streets were empty that night, and I felt the same way inside. What the hell was I doing wrong?

A few days later, I went off to my part time job at a concert venue that I had been working at the past year and a half. Dave Matthews Band was in town, and it was going to be a long day. Ravenna had plans to go out that night to a bar not far from the venue. She assembled four of her friends for a 'Girls' night,' which was most likely going to consist of binge drinking, vomiting, and Whataburger.

"Maybe you can stop by and see me at work before you head out?" I asked.

"I'm sorry, I can't. I won't have enough time," Ravenna said.

I asked this question mid-afternoon, so I know that she was bull-shitting me.

"Ok. Let me know if you need a ride home. I'll be working late." I offered.

"I will. I love you," she calmly said.

Before the show started, there were thousands of people funneling into the front gates of the venue. I couldn't tell you how many couples I saw. A lot of them were holding hands, kissing, and hugging each other. They looked happy, and I envied them.

Ravenna and I were once lovebirds, but now it seemed that she was slowly distancing herself from me. I couldn't find an answer for her behavior. I thought we were in love, but maybe she was just putting on an act until the time was right to let me go. I felt she was using me to erase her troubled past. I thought I was helping her, but quite possibly, I was only temporary.

Once the show was over, the drunk and stoned masses filed out like a herd of cows. Our job was to make sure they safely made it out of the parking lot while under the influence. After all of our duties were done, it was around 2am, which was the same time that all the nightclubs shut down.

I clocked out and headed back to my apartment to crash for the evening. I took a hot shower to wash all the garbage juice off my skin. I went into my room to get ready for bed. I looked over at my phone, and it was blank. There were no text messages or calls from Ravenna. It was 3am, and I began to worry about her.

I called her and she didn't answer. I sent her a text, but there was no response. I became frantic.

Like a mad man, I got in my car and drove to the club Ravenna went to that night. I didn't know what exactly I would find. I knew she drove that night, so even if I did find her car there it wouldn't really answer any questions. Jealousy and fear took control of the wheel, and I was shaking. I kept driving as my stomach began to turn.

I pulled up to the nightclub. I had been there a few times, but I despised places like this. Not only because I always walked out of there broke-as-shit, but the type of people that went to this club were all douchebags and golddiggers.

The parking lot was located behind the club. I pulled in and slowly drove down the empty side street. The hair on the back of my neck stood up as I was pulling around the corner to see if her car was still there. I felt like a stalker.

I'm sure Dateline NBC was filming me for their next investigative report titled, 'Creepers in the Night.'

Sitting towards the back of the empty lot was Ravenna's white Corolla. I drove over to examine the vehicle for any foul play.

There was no one was inside the vehicle, and multiple scenarios began to enter my head.

Maybe she got a cab? Maybe one of her girlfriends drove her home? Or maybe she went home with another guy?

I know I was expecting the worst too soon, but after being burned before, it felt like a logical conclusion.

I decided to go back home and try to get some sleep. There was nothing I could do, except wait for a phone call.

I couldn't sleep the entire night. The thought of Ravenna with another man made me nauseated and angry. I shouldn't ever have to feel this way about the woman that I love.

The next morning, there was still no contact from her. I wanted to call her so bad, but I knew I couldn't give her the upper hand. I was on the defensive, and my blast shield was up waiting for a relationship bomb to go off.

About midday, I received a call, but it wasn't from Ravenna. It was from my good friend Cody.

"Hey, man, what are you doing today?" he asked.

"I'm off today so I have no plans," I replied.

"Want to meet up for drinks? I'm in the area."

"Absolutely, man. That sounds great!"

We met up at an outdoor patio pub. We sat at the bar, ordered a bucket of beer, and also some food to shove down our gullets.

Nothing like hot wings and extreme nachos to promote a healthy colon.

"Juddy, I need to tell you something. Last night, I was at a night club and Ravenna was there," he said.

"Yeah. She was with some of her girlfriends last night," I replied.

"No. She wasn't. She was with her ex-boyfriend the whole night. They were making out and humping each other on the dance floor. Ravenna went home with him."

"Are you fucking serious?"

"Dead serious, dude."

I began to slip into a depressive state laced with anger. My worst nightmare had come true. Cody then began to divulge the background of Ravenna's ex.

He was the biggest cocaine dealer in town.

Go figure.

He dated Ravenna for months and cheated on her twice. He was the one who got Ravenna hooked on cocaine and was also a steroid freak.

He sounded like a pretty swell guy.

We started to drown ourselves in beer and quickly switched to the angry man's drink, whiskey. I was trying as hard as I could to hold back the tears and the pain. I couldn't let her win. I had to be strong. My phone died while I was at the bar or else I would have called and verbally destroyed Ravenna. Instead, Cody and I rang up a $200 bar tab and we were shitfaced.

Cody's girlfriend came to pick us up. Once I got in the car, I started to cry like a little bitch. I couldn't hold it back anymore. It was all pouring out of me. I apologized over and over to Cody and his girlfriend during the ride home for my breakdown.

Once they dropped me off at my apartment, I thanked both of them for what they did for me. I walked in and went out on the balcony. I started to do some heavy meditating. The meditating quickly turned into a whiskey coma on one of my lawn chairs.

The sun woke me up the next morning. The fresh morning air made me sick. I went inside to lie down on my bed to try to recover from the night of debauchery. My head felt like it had been crushed and the smell of whiskey was all over my clothes. Before I crashed, I plugged my phone in to charge.

I awoke from the alcoholic slumber a few hours later to find that I had five missed calls from Ravenna. She didn't leave any voicemails or text messages. After I got out of bed, I called Ravenna and she answered.

These were her exact words: "By now I'm sure you know that I've cheated on you. I'm very sorry for what happened. I had every intention of breaking up with you before this happened. I don't think we should be together anymore."

"Go fuck yourself! I never want to see you again!" I yelled.

I hung up before she spewed out any more bullshit.

What planet did this evil creature come from?

I had to get away before something bad happened. We lived in a small town, and I was bound to run into her somewhere. I called one my best friends, Nathan, who I had known my whole life.

I asked, "Nathan, I don't have a lot of money but I need to get away. Can I crash with you this weekend?"

Nathan responded, "Of course buddy. You are more than welcome."

I packed up a bag as fast as I could and took off.

Nathan lived about three hours away, so I cranked up the music and hauled ass. The entire ride, I was deep in thought about the darkness that resided within the woman I once loved. I was infuriated with Ravenna for destroying everything we had for one night of adulterous cocaine sex.

Who knows how many times that son-of-a-bitch plowed her while we were together?

There was a horrible taste in my mouth. I had been dating a piece of filth the whole time. The pieces of the puzzle were finally coming together in a devastating way.

Ravenna had used me to prove to her parents that she can have a healthy relationship with a good man. I was simply in the presence of her parents to make her seem like she was something that she was not. I was just a pawn in Ravenna's scheme to win her parents' affection back until she got off with that asshole.

The gravity of cheating will always be too heavy to bare. It makes you want to explode in rage against the one who betrayed you.

I put my heart into this relationship, and she ripped it the fuck out. I did everything humanly possible to make her happy, except give her an eight ball of cocaine.

It was over, and I was an emotional wreck. Depression became my close friend who sat next to me at every bar I began to frequent to drown the pain. I was finding it harder to hold myself together. My confidence had crumbled, and I began to feel like I was just not good enough.

How will I ever rebuild my strength from this? When will this emotional torture end?

Relationship Report:

Pros	Cons
• Kind	• Cocaine Junkie
• Long Legs	• Cheater
• Tan Skin	• Addicted to Assholes
• Ghetto Booty	• Liar
• Spontaneous	• Ugly on the Inside

Total Time Lost	1 year, 1 month
Hours of Unpaid Labor	120
Cheated?	Yes
Emotional Trauma (On a Scale of 1 to 10)	7
Sex Life	Average
Physical Abuse	No

Total Montary Loses: $5,395.00

Dinner Dates: 4x per month @ $60 per date

Special Occasion Dates: 1x every 6 months @ $150.00 per date

Gifts (Holidays and Anniversaries): 6x per year @ $100.00 per gift

Commuting Gas Consumption: $1,200 per year.

Chapter 6-Sydnie: 'The Freshman Snake'

Months went by, as I attempted to drag myself out of my sad and lonely reality. I tried to stay busy with school, hockey, and the fraternity. My main focus was improving my grades.

Working my way through summer school, I managed to pull up my GPA and decrease my excessive drinking.

After about six months, I was finally feeling somewhat human again, but getting back in the dating game again could have been dangerous.

My major in college was Criminal Justice. I was required to take six science classes in order to complete my degree. The worst science class I took hands down was Geography.

I'll probably never use this fucking subject for the rest of my life.

On the first day of school, the students walked into the classroom knowing that this would be one excruciating hour and a half. Upon entering the musty auditorium, I happened to notice a gorgeous girl sitting towards the front. She had brown hair and deep blue eyes.

I tried not to stare but sometimes you must take a moment and enjoy beauty. Like a nice oil painting.

I didn't want to be a douchebag and hit on her the very first day of school. I put a stop to all female advances and waited patiently.

Our professor was this forty-year-old guy with a pocket protector and suspenders. Even though he was a science professor, he did not comprehend that humans needed to urinate periodically throughout the day. Every time someone got up to use the restroom, he would flip shit.

For all the college professors out there, you need to chill out. We cannot control when we need to take a piss. It's college for God's sake. Most of us are either hungover or still drunk when we show up to class. Give us a break.

About halfway through the semester in class one day, the blue-eyed girl got up and decided to go to the bathroom. As soon as she began to walk out of class, the teacher stopped his lecture.

He blurted out, "I'm sorry. Am I boring you?"

In a soft voice she replied, "No, sir. I just need to go to the restroom."

"You should've done that before class."

Her face turned bright red, and she walked out of the classroom completely embarrassed. The poor girl didn't even want to come back into class, so she sat outside until it was over. Once class ended, I grabbed her backpack to bring to her. I walked out into the hallway and found her sitting on a bench by herself.

I walked up to her and said, "Is this yours?"

She said, "Yes. Thank you so much. I was so terrified to go back in there."

"Yeah what a dick professor, right?"

Right as I said that, our professor was walking directly behind me. He stopped all of a sudden and glared at me.

He asked, "What did you just say?"

I replied, "Oh, nothing. I could care less about you. I'm more interested in asking this pretty lady on a date."

The professor took a long hard look at me and kept walking.

I mean really what the hell was he going to do? Give me detention?

"How about that date?" I asked.

"Yes. I would love to," she replied.

Her name was Sydnie. She was a freshman who had just broken out of her high school cocoon. She was short with light skin and chocolate brown hair. She seemed innocent and perhaps she was a decent human being with kindness in her heart.

Probably not, but we'll see.

I took Sydnie to this nice Italian restaurant one Friday night. It was located on a small river walk area about thirty minutes from town. I picked her up at the freshman dormitory, which made me feel a little bit like a creep. Sydnie was nineteen and I was twenty-one. There wasn't a huge gap in age, but just enough to make me feel like a criminal.

She had on a silk top with jeans and heels. Her hair was up, and she had big hoop earrings on. She looked exquisite…for a teenager.

Once we were seated at the restaurant, I wanted to get to know Sydnie a little better. I asked her a series of questions like I was interrogating her.

The real questions I wanted to ask were: A. Are you a cheater? B. Do you use drugs? C. When are you going to fuck me over?

Of course, I wasn't about to scare the shit out of her.

"Are you enjoying college so far?" I asked.

"Yes! I love it! I'm having a blast!" she replied.

"Order whatever you want! Everything at this place is amazing."

"Thank you. I just like spaghetti."

She was a cheap date, and I wasn't complaining one bit.

Sydnie also had a great sense of humor, and I thoroughly enjoyed being around her. I was also impressed with her manners.

Sydnie said, "Thank you so much for dinner. Do you want to split the bill?"

I replied, "Absolutely not. This is my treat."

Offering to help pay was something new for me. For the first time, I had met someone who was as polite as I was and it was quite refreshing. The night was a success, and afterwards, we headed back so I could drop her off at her dorm.

After that night, we started to hit it off and began to see each other regularly.

Sydnie and I were very compatible. I enjoyed every minute with her. We were spending time watching re-runs of our favorite TV show 'The Office.' Other times, we were lazy all day in our pajamas around my apartment. We would also have movie marathons, pizza nights, and game nights. It was the most casual relationship I had ever been in, and it felt good.

I didn't want to ruin a good thing, so I didn't make any sudden moves in the bedroom just yet. We kissed and fooled around every now and then, but it was nothing to brag to my buddies about. I wanted to make sure that I did things right. Maybe if I waited for the right time to be sexually intimate, I would have better luck with the relationship.

After about three months of dating, the special time had come. It happened one night after we had finished a nice homemade dinner that I had prepared for us. It was almond crusted chicken, bacon wrapped asparagus, and garlic mashed potatoes.

Sydnie said, "No guy has ever cooked for me."

I happily replied, "There's plenty more meals where that came from."

The mood was right, and we had a few cocktails already inside of us.

Alcohol will always be a key player in the game of love.

We walked into my bedroom. I lit a few candles, and put on some smooth jazz music to make things romantic.

Sydnie chuckled, "Can we listen to something else besides elevator music?"

I embarrassingly replied, "What type of music would you prefer?"

"Do you have any Marilyn Manson?"

I had no idea we were going to be sacrificing small animals to Satan this evening. This could go very well or horribly wrong.

"Um…Sure!"

The first song that came on was 'Personal Jesus.'

How fitting.

There was one minor detail that Sydnie neglected to mention before the sexual festivities began. After some basic foreplay, the moment came for my grand entrance. I proceeded to enter her magical kingdom, but there was something at the front gate attempting to stop me from entering. It was some sort of blockade. After about three attempts to gain access, I paused all 'pelvical thrusting.'

I calmly said, "Sydnie, I'm having a hard time getting inside of you."

She replied, "Oh I'm so sorry. I totally forgot. I have a tampon in."

What the fuck? Let me get this straight. You're telling me that Sydnie forgot about the one time of the month where she suffers from cramping, bloating, sore breast, water retention, pelvic pressure, backache, food cravings, mood swings, irritability, headaches, and fatigue? Not to mention that she has a cotton spaceship parked in her vaginal loading bay?

I guess I had found the only female on this earth that was immune to the menstrual cycle. I should be so lucky.

Sydnie then said, "Well, it's ok. I can just take it out."

As much as I would like to have some marinara sauce on my breadstick…I'll pass.

I replied, "Let's just wait. I'm kind of full, and I don't feel so well."

That was the only thing I could think to say during the sexually awkward moment. We called it a night after the strange revelation.

After the first failed encounter, our sex life became much better. I was finally able to gain access and provide satisfaction for the both of us. I should have caught on by her bedside musical taste but Sydnie was pretty damn aggressive in the bedroom. I would often see bite marks and scratches all over my body the morning after. It was like I was having cage match fights with a tiger. I quickly invested in some aloe, but most of the time, Sydnie would reopen my previous wounds during the next round in the sack.

She was a freshman in college, but had a Ph.D. in anatomical stimulation. Sydnie would put me into positions that would make Cirque du Solei dancers look like shit. I was fairly certain that my muscles were getting torn left and right.

One thing that was a bit frightening was that she would often grunt like an ogre during sex. Her voice would sometimes be deeper than mine.

She would angrily growl, "IT'S MY TURN NOW! LET ME GET ON TOP! GRRRRRRR!"

I was afraid to say no. I had to tell her to keep her voice down because eventually, my roommates began to hear the loud noises throughout the apartment. It sounded like I was banging an angry gorilla.

Sydnie and I had now been dating for about six months. Things were going better in this particular relationship than the last two, so I was quite optimistic. I thought I was finally well on my way to having a good, healthy, and solid relationship.

We spent almost every other day together, and we never had any fights. We got along quite well, and we were growing each day as a couple.

It was wintertime, and it was getting cold outside. There were even days filled with snow, which we both never experienced before.

Sydnie would say, "I don't want to go to class. It's freezing outside."

I asked her, "Why don't you have any jackets to wear?"

She told me she left them at home, and she wasn't going to be able get them until she went back to visit her family for Christmas. I knew that this was unacceptable.

One day Sydnie came over to my apartment after school, and I told her to get in the car. She had no idea what was going on. I then took her to a JC Penny store.

When we walked in, I said, "Pick out any jacket you want as long as it's in the winter sale section."

Sydnie exclaimed, "This is such a great surprise! I can't thank you enough, Juddy!"

She picked out a nice black pea coat, and was finally able to stay warm on her walks to class.

We both went our separate ways for the Christmas break. Neither one of us were quite ready to meet each other's parents. We were taking things slow and knew that soon we would be getting more serious with our relationship. During the break, I talked to her every day on the phone. Even though she was over two hundred miles away, our companionship stayed strong.

Once school started back up, we were finally back together and things were going really well. I was happy with Sydnie and our compatibility couldn't have been better. I had never been this relaxed with a woman. I felt that I could be myself in front of her and not have a care in the world.

We mostly hung out with a core group of friends, and there were about twenty of us. Most of them included friends of mine, but Sydnie had friends from high school who I had gotten to know pretty well. One of Sydnie's friends was a goofy bastard named, Dustin. He had a big nose, big ears, and a high-pitched laugh. He was essentially a clown without makeup.

As soon as I met him, I could easily tell that he had a vested interest in Sydnie. Maybe it was the drool spilling out of his mouth when he saw Sydnie in a low-cut shirt. Or maybe it was the awkward way he would hug her closely to make sure Sydnie's boobs were pressed up against his chest for an extended period of time.

It was like two warm pillows that provided comfort and security...sick bastard.

Not to mention the constant creepy 'Facebook' posts on Sydnie's profile.

"Hey, beautiful! Have a good day," one of the posts read.

I never felt threatened, but it did make me feel uncomfortable.

Spring Break was coming up fast. Sydnie and I wanted to do something fun for the week-long binge-drinking extravaganza. We decided to travel to one of the most cliché college spots, Cancun, Mexico.

On campus, they were offering deals for big groups to go for discounted prices. We quickly assembled a small militia of partygoers. There were about fifteen of us, and we all signed up. It was mostly my buddies with their girlfriends as well as some of Sydnie's friends, including Dustin.

I was a bit hesitant about letting bozo on board, but we needed him for the extra discount.

Sydnie didn't have a job or money, so I picked up the tab for both of us. At first, she didn't want me to pay her portion.

She said, "I don't want you to feel obligated in any way."

I told her, "This is my gift to you! I want you to come with me."

Sydnie smiled and hugged me.

"Thank you so much, Juddy!"

We booked our flight and were ready for a wild time. I was excited to spend this trip with Sydnie. We had never really gone on any type of vacation, so this was going to be nice.

Two weeks later, we took a plane to Cancun. When we arrived, we were greeted with a shuttle service that took us to our final destination. Our group had rented a beach house near the city. It was a two-story cabana with a large back patio and an amazing interior. The kitchen had everything we needed to cook, and we were loaded with alcohol.

Sydnie and I rushed in quickly to find the best room in the house. As soon as we found the one we wanted, I threw Sydnie on the big wooden framed bed like a king with his new queen. Our clothes flew off fast and we cordially broke in the bed. No grunting was allowed.

Most of the couples had rooms to themselves, while a few of the loners such as Dustin, had their own rooms. It was going to be our home away from home for the week, and it was perfect.

The first couple of days were filled with alcohol induced destruction and small amounts of sleep. The inside of the house slowly began to look like a nuclear bomb had exploded. Each day, we would drink until the sun came up. Once it was daybreak, we recharged our batteries and fed ourselves for about two hours. Our meals consisted of the three cornerstones of any nutritious hangover meal: Bagel Bites, Ramen noodles, and Hot Pockets. These foods were sometimes paired with Doritos or Cheez-its. We would then start up the alcoholic engines once again. We felt like shit, looked like shit, but had the time of our lives.

One afternoon, Sydnie and I took a long walk down the shoreline to hit up a taco stand.

Sydnie said to me, "If it wasn't for you I wouldn't be here right now. Thank you so much, Juddy."

I told her, "I wouldn't have come unless you were with me."

The days at the beach were probably the best. By noon, there would be spring breakers from one side of the beach to the other. Alcohol was flowing all over the place, and the party never stopped.

During most of the trip, Sydnie was in her two-piece. She was definitely one of the best looking girls out on the strand. There were many guys who had their eyes on her, but I wouldn't let the jealousy get to me. I was proud to be her boyfriend.

Although. There was one guy in particular who began to bother me.

Fucking, Dustin.

He wouldn't take his eyes off of Sydnie for one second. I think I even saw him lick his lips a few times. I knew that it must have been killing him inside knowing that at the end of the night, Sydnie was in my bed and not his. I sort of felt sorry for the poor bastard.

It was not until the last couple of days that I began to notice some mild flirtatious behavior between Dustin and Sydnie. They were always taking shots together, and he was waiting on her hand and foot. There was also poking and tickling between the two.

I asked Sydnie, "Why is Dustin touching you so much?"

Sydnie replied, "Oh he's innocent. He is just a good friend. That's all."

It wasn't anything intense, but I could definitely tell that something fishy was going on. I kept thinking that there was no way Sydnie would leave me for him. He didn't have anything to offer her except permanent servitude and some ugly ass children.

We all decided to spend that last night at the beach house playing drinking games rather than going out on the strand. For some reason, I wasn't feeling too well that night. It either had to be the continuous liquor funneling, the lack of sleep, or all the shitty food.

Midway through the night of drinking games, I decided to go into our room to lie down for a bit.

Sydnie asked, "Do you need me to come in there with you?"

I replied, "Just meet me in the room whenever the game is over."

"Ok, I will. Love you."

Once I got into the room, I lied down and it was only about ten minutes until I just flat passed out. I then slipped into a deep alcoholic hibernation.

I didn't wake up until the crack of dawn the next morning. The sun was beginning to rise, and the morning fog was rolling in. Everything was pretty normal…except for one thing.

Sydnie was NOT in bed with me.

The naive side of me was thinking maybe she was just in the bathroom. However, I had fallen asleep on the top comforter of the bed, and it hadn't been pulled down or moved in any way. Fear rapidly began to rush through me. I didn't have time to comprehend what might have actually happened. I had just woken up, and my cognitive skills were not yet activated.

I began to do some investigative work. There were no signs of forced entry. The door was closed but it was unlocked. I moved out into the hallway and noticed that all of the bedroom doors were closed. After a closer examination, they all appeared to be locked.

The dining and living areas of the house were completely empty with the exception of a few beer cans and vomit in the kitchen sink.

There's nothing like the smell of barf in the morning.

The next area I examined was the deck outside overlooking the beach. Adjacent to the deck were four of the rooms, which all had windows facing the ocean. One of the rooms was mine so obviously that was ruled out. The next window down was my buddy, Kyle and his girlfriend's room. I was able to see inside, and it was only the two of them in the room.

All of a sudden, my gut instinct kicked in, and I realized that the next window over was none other than Dustin's room. Immediately, I knew something was wrong. The only way to know for sure was to look inside. The blinds were closed, but there was a small space in the middle that I could see through. What I saw inside that room would forever be burned into my retinas. As I peeked inside, I saw Dustin and Sydnie. They were cuddling together, sleeping naked in the bed.

What the fuck?

I knew that the scene inside of that room would haunt me forever. There were two things I regrettably will never forget. Number one was the terrible acne that Dustin had on his neck and back. He really needed to invest in some acne medication or stop using steroids. Number two was the sight of Sydnie next to Dustin sporting some significant side boob action. I was about to spontaneously combust in anger, and something terrible was about to happen.

I decided to get the hell out of there and take a long walk on the beach. I had no idea how far I was going. I was just aimlessly wandering down the shoreline. I was deep in thought and engulfed in rage. Not only did she sleep with that circus freak, but she did it two fucking doors down from me.

If that is not sinister,r then I don't know what is.

While walking down the shoreline, I finally picked a spot and sat down. I closed my eyes and just listened to the crashing waves for a while. I was trying to reduce the anger that was building up inside me. I was out there for a solid two hours, and I knew I eventually had to make it back to catch our departing flight.

After much hesitation, I took a long walk back to the beach house. The whole way, I was contemplating how to deal with this dreadful situation. I came up to the back door, took a deep breath, and walked inside.

It was around 9am, and everyone was moving around. Most of my friends were in the kitchen cooking breakfast. Sydnie was nowhere to be found.

I had no idea if anyone in the house knew about what had happened. Everyone seemed to be acting normal.

I then walked into my room, and guess who was sitting at the foot of my bed?

The one and only…spring break slut.

Sydnie asked me, "Where did you go?"

I replied, "Doesn't matter. Why weren't you in bed with me last night?"

By the squeamish look on her face, I could tell her tiny brain was working as fast as it could to come up with a believable story.

This should be good.

She idiotically explained, "Well, we were all playing drinking games and having a good time. After the game was over, everyone headed to bed. Dustin and I kept drinking. We went into his room just to hang out. I guess I must have fallen asleep because I was tired. Nothing happened at all. I swear."

I found it hard not to laugh at the terrible performance.

I asked, "Would you like to try this again?"

Sydnie said, "You know I love you and that I would never cheat on you."

This is pathetic.

Before Sydnie was able to dig her grave any deeper, I began to expose the truth to her delusional mind.

I said, "I saw you and Dustin together in bed…naked."

I could instantaneously see the shame running down her face in the form of tears.

I yelled, "What the fuck is wrong with you?"

Sydnie wouldn't say anything. She remained silent and not a single word exited her mouth, even though last night it was probably full of dick.

I said, "This is the end for you and me. I now see you for the snake that you are. You destroyed our relationship for one night with that fucking idiot. When we get back home, I never want to see you again."

Sydnie and I didn't speak a single word to each other for the rest of the trip.

Part of me wanted to beat the ever-living shit out of Dustin, but most of my aggression was channeled toward Sydnie. That same day, we flew out to go back home. I had to switch seats on the airplane before we took off because there was no way I was getting anywhere near her for the six hour flight.

When we got back, Sydnie hitched a ride with one of her girlfriends, and I took off on my own. That was by far the worst spring break I ever had.

Arriving back at school the next week, word had traveled fast about what had happened to me. I had many people come up to me on campus with sympathetic words of wisdom, but the sting of her venom was still burning.

Once again, I was the dumbass. I thought things were going great between us. I felt like I was right back where I started. I thought for sure that with my polite demeanor and kind heart, I would hopefully find a woman who would never take advantage of me. It seemed that once these girls got me right where they wanted me, they pulled the trigger, and killed everything.

I was broken inside once again. It was hard trying to put myself back together after being ripped apart over and over. I knew that sooner or later, I would be damaged beyond repair. It was only a matter of time before the growing depression took over my life.

How could it possibly get any worse than this?

Relationship Report:

Pros	Cons
•Appreciative	•Sinisiter
•Considerate	•Cheater
•Deep Blue Eyes	•Liar
•Aggressive in the Bedroom	•Knifing
•Super Casual	•Poisonous

Total Time Lost	10 months
Hours of Unpaid Labor	75
Cheated?	Yes
Emotional Trauma (On a Scale of 1 to 10)	9
Sex Life	Above Average
Physical Abuse	No

Total Montary Loses: $5,720.00

Dinner Dates: 4x per month @ $60 per date

Special Occasion Dates: 1x every 6 months @ $150.00 per date

Gifts (Holidays and Anniversaries): 6x per year @ $100.00 per gift

Spring Break Trip: $3,000.00

Chapter 7-Gretchen 'The Psychotic Gremlin' Part 1

I didn't want anything to do with women for a while. I stepped back and began to focus my attention on school. The fall semester of my senior year in college began, and I was on track to graduate the following May. Before the hockey season started in October, I was elected to the Captain position for the team. I felt quite honored to accept the role, but I knew it was going to take up a bunch of my time.

I was a bit of a 'shut-in' during the fall and winter months. I hardly ever went out to the bars and never even tried to date anyone. I attempted to stay occupied in order to keep my mind off of my broken heart. I became secluded from the college scene and very rarely showed my face at any social gatherings. I was attempting to hide the pain I had suffered through, and I didn't want anyone to see me in that state of mind.

I didn't enjoy being alone. All I wanted was companionship. I had no idea it would be this hard to find.

Once winter break came around, I knew couldn't hide from the world forever. I knew I had to get back in action in order to salvage any remaining experiences during my final year in college.

Every spring, our fraternity hosted a campus fundraiser. The charity event included the participation of all the sororities on campus.

It was one of the best times during the year, and all the proceeds were donated to the Children's Miracle Network.

Every sorority would be competing against each other in numerous athletic and philanthropic events. They included tug of war, flag football, a talent show, and a canned food drive. Each sorority was granted three fraternity members to participate as coaches during the athletic events. I had the privilege of being chosen as a coach for one of the sororities.

I got to know a lot of girls while competing with them. They were fun to be around and also very attractive. I knew that being surrounded by females, I was bound to fall for at least one of them. I had to be strong and keep my guard up, because my failure rate with women was obviously extremely high.

One of the final events of the week was the drag queen contest. Each sorority picked one of their coaches to dress up like a woman and perform a dance on stage. Of course, I was chosen for the embarrassing task.

I had an entourage of five girls assigned to me. Their job was to teach me a specific dance routine and transform me into a woman. I was insanely nervous, and I knew I had my work cut out for me. The dance that was chosen was none other than 'Thriller' by Michael Jackson. There was no way I was even coming close to nailing that epic dance. To make matters worse, I was required to wear a tight black dress, a bra, a wig, and high heels. On top of that, all body hair on my face, arms, legs and chest had to be removed.

This was going to suck.

One of the girls in the group that was assisting in my transformation was named Gretchen. She was in charge of my makeup. She was short with long blonde hair. She had brown eyes and a slim figure, which was accompanied by twig-like arms and legs. At first, I thought she was malnourished, but she was just skinnier than the previous girls I had dated. Unlike the other girls in the group, Gretchen was very quiet and shy. At times it felt like I was talking to a piece of wood. Once I got to know her a little bit better, she began to be more talkative.

On the night of the contest, I went over to the sorority house to get ready. I was scared shitless when I walked in the door. I went into the kitchen area to sit down and get ready for my makeover.

Gretchen walked in with another girl and said, "Are you ready?"

I replied, "Absolutely not, but let's do this!"

The girls both laughed.

I asked Gretchen, "Is there any way I could get a drink?"

She said, "Yes, of course!"

She sent one of the girls out to find me a 'drag queen cocktail.' A few of the girls from upstairs came down to see the work in progress. Everyone that walked in the kitchen began to laugh hysterically.

Finally, a few of the girls arrived with my drink. They handed me a massive forty ounce Sonic mixed drink.

"Drink this whole thing, and you'll be good to go!" one of them said.

I guzzled the booze bomb in about five minutes. The girls were giggling the whole time I was drinking it.

I said. "That was tasty. What was in that?"

One of the girls said, "About 50% blue Powerade slush and 50% Everclear."

Holy shit! What have I done? I'm fucked.

After Gretchen finished my makeup, which included blush, eyeliner, and lipstick I began to practice the dance. Midway through practice, things started to become blurry. The Everclear was quickly seeping into my nerve endings. It was starting to severely affect my motor skills. I was having trouble walking, especially with six-inch heels on.

After a few failed attempts at performing the dance, our time was up, and we had to head to the club for the event. Gretchen carefully guided me outside into her car.

I looked like a crippled runway model.

Once we arrived at the event, the girls from the sorority I was representing were buying me shots left and right. They wanted to make sure I was relaxed before my dance routine. About two hours in, I could barely stand up straight. Gretchen was my caretaker and was doing her best to hold me upright until show time.

Suddenly, it was my time to shine. I drunkenly climbed on stage, introduced myself, and the performance began. Due to my blood alcohol level being in the double digits, what actually transpired on that stage was a mystery to me. My memory was obliterated by pure grain alcohol, and I had no recollection of the entire night.

I woke up at noon the next day in my bed. I had no idea how the hell I got there, but I knew one thing. I had to take a piss. As I stumbled into the bathroom, I looked in the mirror and I saw one of the most disgusting things I had ever seen.

I looked like a white trash crack wore. I still had lipstick on which was smudged all over my face. My mascara had gotten wet and was smeared all over my cheeks like I had been crying. One of the fake eyelashes was hanging down from my eyelid, and the bra was still attached.

What the fuck happened last night?

Gretchen and some of the girls came over to bring me some food. They also got me four bottles of Pedialyte to help me recover. They sat me down and filled me in on my performance the night before. It felt like an intervention.

They said once I got up on stage, I miraculously nailed the dance. There were just a few mistakes, but the judges awarded me the first place prize. Once the trophy was given to me, I began to cry for no apparent reason.

I guess it was a captivating moment for me.

Apparently I also made several advances on Gretchen during the ride home. I told her she was the most beautiful girl I had ever seen among other things. God only knows what else spewed out of my mouth that night. I was completely embarrassed.

I pulled Gretchen aside before the girls left. This was my final semester at college, and I didn't want to have any regrets

I said, "I would like to take you out for dinner next week. I feel terrible about last night, and I owe you one."

She replied, "Of course. I mean it's the least you can do…I'm just kidding."

A few days later, I picked Gretchen up for dinner. On the car ride there, she really didn't say too much. I was trying to start up some conversation, but the wheels were not turning.

I took us to a sushi place in town.

I asked her, "What type of sushi rolls would you like?"

Gretchen said, "California rolls are good."

We ordered a stack of rolls and some shrimp fried rice. Once again, I tried to start up a conversation, but it was like trying to converse with a brick wall. She didn't reciprocate very much at all, and I found myself rambling multiple times. I have always been a conversationalist.

I do not like silence...except when I sleep.

Most of her responses were only one word. It was, "Yeah, sometimes, or maybe" throughout the entire night. I was wondering if there was any sign of a personality inside that small body of hers. Once the food arrived, we started to dig in. There was hardly anytime for chewing. We scarfed down the grub rapidly, and both of us felt pretty full afterwards.

I wanted to take things slow this time around.

I told Gretchen, "Since we both have an early class tomorrow, do you want to call it an early night?"

Gretchen replied, "Yeah that sounds good. Thank you for dinner, Juddy. I had a great time."

That was the longest sentence she spoke all evening. I needed to go home and regroup to see how I could exfoliate Gretchen's personality out of her. Surely there would be some sort of active dialogue from her in future conversations.

For the first few weeks, I was treading lightly until I really got to know her. It was sometimes hard to gauge her feelings. I mean I guess she liked me, or otherwise she would have stopped seeing me.

After about a month, we began to date each other exclusively. The common phrase 'opposites attract' described our relationship perfectly. I was the loud, social, and outgoing one. She was the mute who occasionally laughed.

After a few days, Gretchen's personality slowly began to surface. I was good at making her laugh and we enjoyed each other's company quite a bit. We were seeing each other almost every day. Most of the time we would go out with friends to the bars and have drinks. Other times, she would come over to my apartment where I would cook us dinner, which I always enjoyed doing. The only two things she knew how to cook were EZ Mac and Bagel Bites. Both equally delicious, but I wouldn't call that 'cooking' by any means.

After dinner we would drink wine, and if I was lucky, we would fool around a bit in the bedroom. Like I said, it was extremely difficult to determine the type of mood Gretchen was in. I was essentially throwing out live bait to see if I could get a little nibble each night we were together.

Gretchen was extremely self-conscious about her body. She was thin and short but top heavy. Her gazongas were larger than average and at times, she had trouble balancing herself on the ground. Migrating to Gretchen's wondrous mountains was quite a challenge. Every time I ventured near that general area, I was immediately denied access. Needless to say, the very first time we had sex was extremely weird.

One night, Gretchen and I were in bed making out. Then we began to dry hump each other like two chimpanzees with nothing to lose, except our clothes of course. During this pre-sex ritual, I attempted to undress Gretchen. She refused to let me take off any of her clothing. With a cool, calm, and collective tone I simply said to her, "This would be a lot easier if we removed our clothes."

She replied, "Just move my clothes out of the way."

She was wearing jean shorts and a T-shirt. It was a rather difficult task to try and maneuver my way past the denim chastity belt. After several attempts, I was finally able to breach the jean barrier wall.

Not only did the finagling of my wiener ruin the romance, but also, Gretchen was just lying there like a dead fish. No emotion, no expressions, and no signs of sexual stimulation were present. My bed sheets were soaked with boredom, and the encounter only lasted about five minutes.

I wonder how much I have to pay for a half nude or fully nude interactive experience?

I did not want to judge Gretchen based on this unfortunate episode. I prayed that the next time around it would be much more pleasurable for the both of us.

My college graduation was right around the corner. I had just been accepted into the police academy and my orientation day was only a few weeks away. My plans were to move about forty miles south from town. That would put me close to the academy, but not very far from Gretchen. The academy was going to be extensive, time consuming, and brutal. It would be the longest six months of my life, so before I graduated college I had to make a choice.

Do I stay with Gretchen hoping that we have a future together? Or do I end it all right now and move on? This decision would either set me on the right path or take me to a very dark place.

We had been together for only about five months. I believed that maybe this was my last chance to find true love. There was a risk involved but I was willing to take it in hopes of a better future.

Gretchen and I both sat down and had a long conversation about our relationship.

I said to her, "Gretchen it will be hard while I'm in the academy, but I am willing to be with you and continue our relationship. I care for you very much, and I think we have a lot of growing to do."

She replied, "I care for you too, and I love being around you. I want us to be able to see each other as much as possible."

"I will do everything in my power to see you every chance that I get, but the academy will take up a lot of my time."

"I'm proud of you for joining the police force, and I will do whatever I can to help you through it."

For the first time, Gretchen was really opening up to me. Only took about half a year, but I knew that she meant every word.

The following week, I finally graduated from college. I only had about two weeks before the police academy began. I tried to make the most of it and spend as much time with Gretchen as I could. I knew that once I entered the academy, things would be very hard on the both of us.

Once the academy began, I was busy nonstop during the week. The days started at 5am and ended at 7pm. There was physical training, classroom lectures, and military style discipline. I didn't quite fit in there, but I was the one that signed up, and I needed to finish what I started.

I spent my weekends driving forty five miles back and forth to visit Gretchen. Often times, she would stay with me at my place, but that was few and far between. It was hard trying to study on the weekends on top of visiting Gretchen, but I enjoyed being with her.

During the first month I was commuting, I immediately felt a sense of bankruptcy. Gretchen had this crazy notion that I had endless amounts of money. I was getting paid next to nothing while in the academy, and I really didn't have a pot to piss in. I would train at the academy Monday through Friday, drive to see Gretchen for the weekend, and barely have enough gas money to get back home.

Don't get me wrong; I was enjoying spending time with Gretchen. We would have a blast together, and for the most part, the long drives were worth seeing the woman that I was steadily falling in love with.

However, there was this one night where something bizarre happened. The dark side of Gretchen was suddenly revealed for the first time. This was something I had never seen before, and I was not prepared for it whatsoever.

Gretchen and I were at the bar one night with some friends. We were there for about fifteen minutes, and she had already guzzled about six shots of random concoctions. She was drunk as a skunk in no time.

Gretchen then began to transform into this strange type of creature. It was a lot like the movie 'Gremlins.'

At first, Gretchen was a nice, cute, and friendly animal. Once liquid was introduced in the form of alcohol, she turned into something evil. She became extremely aggressive, confrontational, and angry. She began to talk shit to other girls who were in rivaling sororities.

She would say things like, "Sucks to suck, bitches!" and "You're such a SLORE," (slutty-whore).

Gretchen had hatred flowing through her veins and there was no stopping it. I had to break up fights and calm her crazy ass down every time I turned my head. It was exhausting and embarrassing at the same time. She was the mastermind behind the sorority shit-storm. Anytime I didn't immediately get involved in one of the many idiotic altercations, she claimed that I was a bad boyfriend because I didn't stick up for her.

How do you defend a psychotic monster with tequila dripping from her fangs?

Towards the end of the night, I said, "Gretchen, we need to leave or they are going to kick you out."

She blurted out, "I would like to see those assholes try."

The bouncers could have probably picked her tiny head up with one hand and tossed her out the front door like a trash bag.

The night ended with me dragging Gretchen out of the bar kicking and screaming.

I guess this is what parents go through with their shitty kids.

I shouldn't have had to put up with any of this bullshit. Gretchen's transformation from girlfriend to goblin had me confused and angry. Of course, once we got home, Gretchen began to cry.

She sobbed, "I'm sorry for everything tonight. I don't know what happened to me."

I know exactly what happened. It was the multiple shots of liquor mixed with sorority bullshit.

I said, "Let's just go to bed and we will talk about it in the morning."

The next day, Gretchen and I discussed in detail about the crazy events the night before. She said that the girls she was fighting with had been talking shit behind her back.

I asked her, "What have they said about you?"

Gretchen mumbled, "I don't know. Just stupid rumors about me."

She apologized to me several times. I forgave her and headed home to go study for a big exam I had coming up. I was praying that I would never see the evil gremlin ever again.

During the academy, Gretchen was very supportive. She would help me study for the numerous tests I had to take. She would also help me shave my head and face for the academy. As a police trainee, they wanted us to look like baby-faced douchebags at all times. I even had to shave at lunch every day because my beard would start to instantly grow back like a Chia Pet drenched in water.

After a grueling six months of police training, I finally graduated the academy in January. I was officially a police officer and was thrown out on the streets to protect and serve...

Does this look like someone who is ready to punish criminals and uphold justice with lethal force? I don't think so.

Here...we...go!

<u>Roll Call</u>
<u>Downtown Police Station</u>
<u>Central Command</u>
<u>5:00am</u>

There I was sitting in my car in the police station parking lot. My hands were shaking and my eyes were twitching. I was scared shitless.

I sat in my car for about thirty minutes collecting my thoughts. I had been in a classroom for six months and now it's go time. I slowly got out of my car and headed into the station. With my shaved head, pale skin, and pressed uniform I was a dead giveaway. At the front desk I signed in and the officer there said, "Good luck today, rookie. Welcome to the gauntlet."

I took the elevator upstairs to head to roll call. I walked into the conference room and there were about twenty five officers there.

One of them goes, "Oh shit. Another rookie. Aren't we lucky?"

The rest of the officers began to laugh and the sergeant came in. He gave his report for the day and gave us our assignments. My training officer that I was going to be riding with was only a year older than me. He had been on the force for two years. His name was Officer Adams.

He grabbed me and said, "Get you gear and let's get a move out."

I quickly picked up my huge duffle bag of police equipment. We made our way to the parking garage, loaded up our squad car, and headed out.

First Call
6:00am
Traffic Accident
Summary:
A thirty-five-year-old jackass in a Porsche was flying down the highway at high speeds. He lost control, flew over the middle divider median, and into a sixty-five year old woman in a suburban. The woman was carried off in a stretcher in critical condition. Meanwhile, the man was claiming that he was going the speed limit the whole time. We wrote him up for failure to maintain lane, speeding, and reckless endangerment.

Second Call
7:30am
Domestic Dispute
Summary:
A homosexual male couple had gotten into a fight at their apartment. There were no punches thrown. Only slaps and scratches. It was a black guy and a white guy.

The black guy was claiming that he caught his boyfriend red-handed giving a blowjob to another guy in the parking lot that morning behind a dumpster. He confronted his boyfriend about it, and they began to fight inside the apartment. The black guy said he had the sexual act on video if we wanted to examine it.

We declined.

There were no visible marks on either individual and no blood was drawn. We told the white guy to find another place to go. We told the black guy to change his locks.

Third Call
9:00am
Domestic Violence
Summary:

We hauled ass to get to the location as quick as we could. We arrived at a rundown apartment complex. We then walked upstairs while passing one fifty-year-old male with a dog that he was taking for a walk. We knocked on the door and a nineteen-year-old girl answered.

She was in tears, had a black eye, and was intoxicated. The girl told us that her father had molested her and beat her that morning. She gave us his description, and we soon realized that it was the same asshole that passed us on the stairs.

We ran downstairs and chased that fucker down. I had to taser the shit out of him to get him to comply with our commands. We arrested him for Domestic Sexual Assault and took him to jail.

Fourth Call
10:00am
Possible Robbery in Progress
Summary:

We hauled ass to this call as well. We showed up at the house, drew our guns, and began to do a search of the house.

Only five hours in to my first day and my gun was already drawn.

While we were upstairs, we heard footsteps coming from the downstairs area. We ran downstairs, cleared the room, and then ran outside. There was no trace of anyone so we cleared the call, filed a report, and moved on.

<u>Fifth Call</u>
<u>11:30am</u>
<u>Suspicious Individual in the Fourth Ward.</u>
<u>Summary:</u>
There were six wards within the city, which were low income government housing areas. The Fourth Ward was one of the worst. It housed many drug dealers, hookers, and ex-cons.

We found a suspicious male walking down the street. He fit the description we were given by the dispatcher. We rolled up, got out of the car, and began to question him. My trainer then wanted me to handcuff and search him. As I was searching him I noticed a MS-13 tattoo on his forearm. The hair on the back of my neck stood up. MS-13 was known as the world's most dangerous gang. We ran his license number and he had an outstanding warrant issued for sexual battery, which was sexual assault with a deadly weapon.

As I was putting him in the car, he saw my nametag and said, "I got my boys watching you right now, Officer Ferguson. Watch your back bitch."

Looks like I won't fucking sleep tonight.

<u>Sixth Call</u>
<u>1:00pm</u>
<u>Disorderly Conduct</u>
<u>Summary:</u>

A half drunk military vet was apparently beating the shit out of an Escalade with a wooden stick at a car wash. When we arrived, the description was completely accurate. We ran up to the man and told him to drop the stick. He got on the ground and we handcuffed him.

The owner of the Escalade told us that after the car had been washed, the old man came out of the woods and began to beat the vehicle with a wooden tree limb. He wanted to press charges.

We arrested the man for public intoxication, damage to private property, and reckless behavior.

I asked the old man why he was attacking the Escalade. He said, "He started it (the vehicle). He's a symbol of greed."

Off to jail he went.

<u>Seventh Call</u>
<u>3:00pm</u>
<u>Suspicious activity in the Fourth Ward...again.</u>
<u>Summary:</u>

There was a call that came in regarding some possible drug dealing at a house in the Fourth Ward. My trainer said that he visits this house a lot for all types of criminal activity. We rolled up fast to the house to catch them off guard. As soon as we pulled up there were four guys outside the house on the front lawn. They all ran inside once they saw us.

All of a sudden I heard three loud pops. They were gunshots. Two of them hit the hood of the car, and there was oil spraying from the engine block. The third shot shattered the passenger side rearview mirror. We both rolled out of the car and got behind the back bumper.

I screamed, "What the fuck do we do now?"

My trainer yelled, "Aim and shoot you dumbass!"

I attempted to take aim and shoot but it was tough with multiple bullets flying past my head. Plus, they had much bigger guns than we did. Our squad car was getting torn to shreds.

My trainer said, "Call for back up now or we're both dead!"

I was scared out of my fucking mind and couldn't even speak on the radio. I began to stutter like an idiot.

I said, "Unit 32 to C-c-c-c-command, we need b-b-b-back up."

My trainer yelled, "Just give me the fucking radio asshole!"

He alerted command of our location. Bullets were still flying all around us. Each and every pop I heard, I prayed that none of them would hit us. Finally, SWAT arrived and took control of the situation.

After some heavy negotiating, the criminals inside surrendered. There were no deaths but I was pretty sure that I had shit myself.

Downtown Police Station
Central Command
_4:30pm_

My first shift as a police officer was over.

After that day, I was ready to call it quits but I had never been a quitter. I had worked so hard to get this job but was it worth my life?

All I wanted to do was protect the public and make a difference. I went ahead and completed my training phase, which was three months. Upon completing my probationary police officer training, I had the option to go solo on patrol.

I thought about my family, Gretchen, and my friends. The thought of losing my life would not escape my mind.

I decided to respectfully decline and resign as a police officer.

It was one of the best decisions I had ever made, and I would never go back.

Chapter 8-Gretchen 'The Psychotic Gremlin' Part 2

Once I resigned, I couldn't find a job for a few months. I had enough money to pay the bills, but only a small amount to continue to visit Gretchen. I spent every dime I had driving up to see her. I loved her, and was giving our relationship my all.

So far, it had been a year and a half with Gretchen. We had been through a lot together, and I felt that we had grown quite a bit. This was the second longest relationship of my life, and in my mind, I felt that it would be the last. I knew that we were happy together and we would become a much stronger couple as time went by.

Unfortunately, as with any relationship, things were not always picture perfect.

Gretchen was at her best when she was sober. When her mind was introduced to the number one root for all female evil, otherwise known as alcohol, she became the gremlin again. The evil creature would only come out of its cave when Gretchen was shitfaced.

A night on the town with Gretchen would normally result in two possible outcomes. Scenario number one would involve Gretchen hammered to start the night off right. She would then act like a maniac bouncing from guy to guy attempting to get free drinks.

She would say to me, "Don't be mad if I flirt with other guys. I'm just saving you money."

Wow. I feel like a broke piece of shit. Thank you for the consideration Gretchen.

She would inevitably get so drunk that I would have to drag her out of the bar like a dead corpse.

Scenario number two would be Gretchen getting shitfaced and she would then begin to chastise me about the women of my past. She would make fun of them and call them names. These were girls that I had dated long before I ever met Gretchen, but it was a small college town, so she knew exactly who they were. I never knew what made her so insanely jealous. Obviously the alcohol played a role, but there had to be something else that was giving birth to her madness.

It was summer time, and Gretchen had three months off from school. She moved back home which wasn't too far from my apartment. We spent nights alone together for a while and it felt good. We would order Chinese takeout, watch movies, and enjoy each other's company. There was no drama and no bullshit. It was great being with her without any outside distractions. It was like when we first met and our chemistry was spot on. We were steadily moving towards the loving couple I wanted us to be.

One night, we decided to drive up to our college town. Gretchen wanted to visit some of her friends that she hadn't seen in awhile. We went to a house party to get things started, and then headed to the bar.

Lord, protect me from evil.

As we walked into the local watering hole, there weren't too many people there just yet. We were able to get drinks pretty fast, and we started pouring them down our throats.

At the bar that night, there was a drink of the day special. It was called 'Jungle Juice.' It was every transparent type of liquor on the alcoholic spectrum and Hawaiian punch. I believe it got the name because it resembled gorilla blood.

Who the hell even knows what that tastes like?

They had four Gatorade jugs with spouts at the bottom for convenience. It was twenty dollars, all you can drink, and we were about to get plastered. We emptied an entire jug of that shit. Our lips and tongues were bright red and we were raging inside the bar…like a bunch of gorillas.

Gretchen was drunk, but thankfully there was no aggressive behavior…yet. We were all having a good time and we shut the place down. Afterwards, we all piled into a few cabs and headed home. Gretchen was quiet on the ride back, too quiet in fact.

"Is everything ok?" I asked.

"We'll talk about it when we get home," she replied.

Oh shit. Was there evil boiling in her blood?

Once Gretchen and I arrived at her townhome, the atmosphere inside was quite chilly. I could see my breath in the air. The walls were darker than usual, and I could sense that something villainous was about to consume the house.

We went into her room to get ready for bed. As soon as we walked into the bathroom to change, Gretchen turned around and began to slap and punch me in the face.

What the fuck is this?

Gretchen was tiny, so the hits didn't have any real brute force to them. The slaps stung, but that's about it. During this beating, she screamed and yelled things like: "Fucking leave now!" "You're such an asshole." "I can't believe you had sex with that slut!"

STOP! Who the fuck is she talking about?

I let her rage unfold through her fists until she ran out of breath.

After the onslaught was complete, Gretchen went into her closet or what I'd like to call 'the doorway to hell' to change clothes.

As much as I just wanted to leave this nightmare, I was too drunk to drive and I wasn't about to sleep in my car. I reluctantly got into bed and prepared myself for another thrashing of Gretchen's psychosomatic aggression. She came out of the closet and got into bed. Then all of a sudden, she grabbed my wiener like it was an Olympic torch.

She yelled in a deep evil voice, "PUT IT INSIDE ME, MOTHERFUCKER!"

I let out a high-pitched scream like a teenage girl in horror film. Not only because was I afraid of what would happen to me if I didn't do what she asked, but her hand was as cold as ice.

Sex was becoming more infrequent in our relationship, so it was hard to say no. Even it if meant making love to a monster from the depths of hell. It was the most ferocious sex I have ever had. She was tossing me around like a fucking rag doll. I didn't have time to take a breath, and she dominated me the entire time.

After the violent sex crazed episode ended, Gretchen fell right asleep. She snored like a wild hog and drooled like a troll the entire night. I couldn't sleep. I was traumatized from head to toe.

Early the next morning, I got up and hopped in the shower. I was hoping the water would cleanse me of all the sins from the night before. After my second baptism, I got out and dried off. I walked back into the room, and Gretchen was staring at me with her typical blank face.

I asked her, "Do you have anything to say about what happened last night?"

Gretchen shrugged at me like a child and said, "Sorry?"

I think I'm dating a woman from another dimension.

I began to explain to Gretchen that what happened last night was completely fucking crazy. Gretchen was claiming that she didn't remember anything that happened after we got home. I found that hard to believe.

I yelled, "You hit me, slapped me, and screamed at me. What the hell is wrong with you?"

Gretchen began to cry. She said, "I'm so sorry. I really don't remember what happened. I feel terrible, Juddy."

I also mentioned to her that as much as I enjoyed having sex with her, I would rather make love to my girlfriend rather than a satanic beast.

What in God's name caused this? There must be something buried within her that was causing this violent maniacal behavior.

I was extremely hesitant to move forward after this atrocious event. Anytime Gretchen's lips touched a shot glass, I immediately began to feel pain.

I wanted to plan a weekend for just the two of us. If we got away from all the negativity and the drama, maybe I could truly evaluate if we should be together. This would give me a chance to talk in depth with her about our relationship and possibly locate the origin of her lunacy.

I went to Gretchen and said, "Hey let's get away for the weekend and go somewhere. Anywhere but here."

She replied, "My dad has a lake house, and it's only about two hours away."

"That's perfect! Are you sure he won't mind?"

"I'm sure it will be fine. Let me just ask him."

Gretchen called her father, and he gave us permission to go. Her father was actually going to the lake house that same weekend with his current girlfriend. Gretchen's parents separated when she was young but I never asked why.

Gretchen asked, "Are you ok with them being there?"

I replied, "Of course. I think it might be time for me to meet your father."

"Ok but just a heads up sometimes my dad can be mean, but he really is a good man."

"What do you mean?"

"He has a temper and a little bit of a drinking problem."

Fucking awesome. Can't wait.

That following weekend, we headed to the lake house. During our drive there, I wanted to ask Gretchen about her parent's divorce but I didn't want to be nosey. I figured if the subject came up we would talk about it. Gretchen never really mentioned anything about her parents to me, and I found that strange.

Was she hiding something?

Once we arrived at the lake house, Gretchen's father greeted us at the front door with his girlfriend.

He said, "Hello there, I'm Gretchen's father and you must be, Juddy."

I replied, "Yes sir. It's a pleasure to meet you."

We all walked into the large wooden cabin. It was very spacious inside with a fireplace and a large outdoor balcony. On the outside of the house there was a large back patio overlooking the lake. There was also a small boat with a dock attached to the property.

Gretchen's father and girlfriend were very welcoming. They showed us to our room, which was upstairs. I didn't want to overstep her father's boundaries, so I asked Gretchen, "Is it okay with your father that we sleep in the same room?"

She replied, "Yeah, it's fine. He doesn't mind at all."

We all changed into our swimsuits and T-shirts. We then hopped onto the boat and headed out to the lake. We drove around the embankment for a bit in order to get into some open water. There was a large inner tube inside the boat that was attached to a long rope. I threw the tube out, jumped in the water with Gretchen, and held on for dear life. Gretchen had trouble hanging on with the increasing boat speed, so I grabbed her life vest and held us both on the tube for as long as I could. We were out there for about three hours, and we were exhausted.

Gretchen's father had already tipped back about seven beers which made me a little nervous. I didn't know exactly how to drive a boat but I may get a crash course if he decides to guzzle any more brews.

He blurted out, "Do you want a beer? I only have about four left."

I said, "Yes sir. Thank you."

He gave one to Gretchen and his girlfriend as well.

We pulled in the tube and began to head back to the lake house. Before we arrived at the boat dock, Gretchen's father gave me a rundown of how to safely help him guide the boat into the docking area. His words were drunkenly slurred throughout the entire conversation. I tried to make out what I could but a lot of it was alcoholic gibberish.

Once we pulled up to the dock, I hopped out of the boat and began to guide it in. All of a sudden, Gretchen's father began to belligerently lash out at me.

He yelled, "What the fuck are you doing that for? You need to be on the other side! What is wrong with you?"

It took so much inner strength to bite my tongue during the stressful moment. Gretchen and her father's girlfriend were completely silent the entire time while I tried to stay calm.

I asked her father, "How far does the boat need to be in?"

He snapped and said, "I told you that earlier dumbass. Weren't you paying attention?"

The docking process was finally over, and the boat was up.

Thank God. What a fucking asshole.

We all headed inside and no one said a single word to each other. I was so pissed at how her father talked to me, but I was trying hard to keep my composure for Gretchen's sake.

This outburst from her father began to shed some light on Gretchen's behavior. Her father followed suit just like his daughter. He got drunk, became angry, and attacked me. The change in his demeanor was instantaneous. He was easy going out on the lake and once we arrived back at the house, he flipped shit.

We all walked inside and had a quick meal. There was nothing but silence at the dinner table. Her father just went about the day as if nothing happened. There was no apology, no sympathy, and no explanation.

Suddenly, I had an epiphany. I began to wrap my brain around the fact that Gretchen, as well as her father, may have some sort of sickness inside of them. I started to feel sorry for Gretchen. Maybe her father genetically passed something down to her? I know inside that small fragile body of hers was the girl that I fell in love with. Maybe Gretchen needed help in order to bring out the kindness in her heart.

I went over to Gretchen and said, "Let's get out of here tonight. I don't feel comfortable here."

She said, "I know, I'm so sorry. Let me talk to my dad and tell him we are heading out."

I grabbed our things and started pack up the car. Gretchen ran out the front door in tears a few moments later.

I asked, "What happened?"

She sobbed, "Let's just get the hell out of here."

"Let's go get a hotel room and have a romantic evening together."

"I would love that."

I got on my phone and found a nice hotel on a river walk area about an hour away. It was an upscale place, located in the heart of the city.

That night we went to a nice Mexican restaurant on the river walk. We got a great spot on the second floor which was overlooking the city skyline. We had some great food and about one too many margaritas. Our hotel was walking distance so we didn't have to drive anywhere. We drunkenly stumbled back to the hotel, laughing and kissing each other the whole way. Once we got in the room, for the first time in a long time, we had a healthy sexual experience without any anger or violence. This was the weekend I was hoping for.

It was just the two of us, without a care in the world.

After a few months working a low-income part time job, I was finally fortunate enough to be offered a full time position at a salt-water pool company. I was hired on for sales, and I was excited about the great opportunity.

Finally, my cash flow was back to normal. Instead of buying Ramen noodles by the crate, I was able to upgrade to real food, which was a luxury for me.

I lived pretty close to my new job, but it was about forty five minutes from Gretchen who was still in college. I would work hard during the week and then leave for the weekend to stay with her.

Sometimes I would drive up on Thursday nights, go out on the town with Gretchen, and then drive back early the next day to work hungover as shit.

Those were some of the worst drives I have ever taken.

When the summer started, I began to work Saturdays. My work schedule began to cut into the time I wanted to spend with Gretchen. I would often try to see her every weekend but sometimes it couldn't be done.

Towards the end of that summer, Gretchen had gone out one evening with some friends to a party. She would always let me know when she got home at night with a text message. It was good to know that when I woke up the next morning, she was home safe.

The next morning I woke up and I didn't have a text or call from her. I began to worry.

I hate being this way. Always walking on eggshells.

The next morning on 'Facebook,' I saw that Gretchen had posted a status update the night before that read, "I love Pikes." The Pikes were a rival fraternity of ours on campus mainly due to the fact that they always started fights with every other fraternity for no apparent reason. Gretchen knew that I wasn't fond of the half-assed mediocre Greek organization, which was most likely why she didn't tell me where exactly she was going that night.

Later that afternoon, I received a disturbing text from Gretchen.

It read, "Hey, I'm really sorry, but I kissed another guy last night."

Are you fucking kidding me?

I immediately called her and of course she didn't have the guts to answer the phone. About an hour later, Gretchen called me crying uncontrollably.

She cried out, "I know you probably hate me right now but it was a mistake. I'm so sorry."

I said, "You got a lot of nerve unraveling this bullshit through a text message Gretchen. You have made a grave mistake."

She began to cry more.

I told her, "You owe me an explanation face to face."

Gretchen packed up her things and drove down to meet me at my apartment that same night. When she showed up, her face was covered in smeared eyeliner. Her eyes we bloodshot red, and her hair looked like a rats nest.

At least run a comb through that shit before you show up looking like a piece of white trash.

She ran up to me. I stopped her before she could wrap those skinny arms around my waist.

I said, "Don't touch me. Let's go inside."

Once we walked into my apartment, she began breaking down and apologizing over and over.

She pleaded, "Please forgive me. I'm so sorry. I didn't mean to hurt you. It was a mistake."

I exclaimed, "What the fuck were you thinking? Do you even give a shit about me at all?"

"Yes. I love you so much and I never want to hurt you again. I know I screwed up, and I'm asking for your forgiveness. Everyone makes mistakes. I'm not perfect, and I'm truly sorry."

"Was it just a kiss?"

"Yes, just a peck on the lips."

"Who was it?"

"Just some guy in the Pike fraternity."

Hopefully it wasn't a kiss on the Pike's pecker.

She said, "You have to trust me. It was only a kiss."

Gretchen began to cry more and more as the conversation went on.

Even though this was a huge fuck-up on her part, I truly did see the remorse in her face. I knew she was telling the truth and speaking from her heart.

She said, "I love you, Juddy, and I want to be with you. You make me so happy, and I will never hurt you again."

I looked deep into Gretchen's eyes. I said, "Now listen to me very carefully. What you did last night destroyed every piece of trust I had in you. I will forgive you, but I will never forget what happened. The only reason why I will continue to see you is because I know we love each other, and I know that you're being honest with me. I know people make mistakes, but if you pull anything like this again. You are a ghost."

Most people might think that a simple kiss doesn't necessarily constitute as cheating. Cheating has always been very black and white for me. Anything that you would not want your significant other to do physically or emotionally with another person would be cheating in my eyes.

I believe that when we are engulfed in the flames of love we sometimes forget who we are and what we deserve. We alter our feelings and mind to believe that we are happy but at times we are not.

Was this the woman I was meant to be with? Do I deserve someone better? Why am I afraid of being alone?

I don't want you to think that I have myself on this tall pedestal. I am in no way the perfect man. I have my flaws like everyone on this earth. I try my very best to make the woman I love happy. Period.

In order to give you a taste of who I was as a boyfriend, I did some digging into depths of my 'Facebook' wall and ran across this post from Gretchen...

Chapter 9- Gretchen 'The Psychotic Gremlin' Part 3

We both tried to repair the emotional damage that was done. Slowly, we began to drift into the loving couple we once were about a year and a half ago. I was still driving back and forth visiting Gretchen every weekend that I could. I was trying to help us survive.

One particular weekend, I was driving up to see Gretchen on a Friday evening. On my way into town, she called me and she sounded upset.

I asked her, "Is everything ok?"

Gretchen replied, "I locked myself out of my room again."

"Do you have a spare key somewhere?"

"It's locked inside my room too."

That was a smart move. What good was a spare key if it's inside the object you want to open?

I told her that we would figure something out when I got there. Before I even pulled up to her house, I got a text from her that said, "I got in."

This can't be good.

As soon as I walked in the door, I looked over at Gretchen's room and saw one of my buddies named Trevor standing in front of the doorway. The door was smashed in half with broken pieces of wood scattered all over the place. I looked at Trevor and said, "What the hell did you do that for?"

He mumbled, "Gretchen told me to do it."

I looked right at Gretchen and said, "Is this true?"

She replied, "Oh, Juddy who cares? It's just a door."

It would only make sense that she wouldn't give a shit because guess who would have to buy a new door and install it?

Her fucking boyfriend that's who.

I sternly said, "Get in the car and let's get this over with."

I took Gretchen with me to the hardware store to buy a new door, new hinges, and a doorknob. It ended up costing me about a hundred bones.

We got back, and I installed the new door without too much trouble. I wanted to make sure she didn't lose her four hundred dollar deposit when she moved out. This idiotic fiasco wasn't the only thing that went wrong that weekend.

The next day, a bunch of us went tailgating for the football game. Gretchen and some of her friends that were with us were underage, so we went to Sonic to get some Route 44 drinks. We would dump half the drink and fill the rest with alcohol. We called it the 'Sonic Switch.'

As with most college towns, lurking around campus there are the Alcoholic Beverage Commission Officers. The duties of an A.B.C. officer were to enforce laws that prevented individuals from drinking underage. They were out in full force that day, and I even warned Gretchen and her friends about them. I told everyone in the car to finish the drinks before we arrived at the tailgate.

Gretchen said, "Juddy, we will be fine. Don't worry about it."

Once we arrived at the tailgate, we went over to my fraternity tent to say hello and get some food. We were there for a few hours just mingling and drinking.

All of a sudden, one of Gretchen's friends came up to me and said, "Gretchen is getting arrested."

Perfect.

I went over to where Gretchen was being detained. She was in handcuffs and being questioned by two officers. I asked the officers what she was arrested for.

One of them said, "Public Intoxication. Now back off or I will arrest you too."

Look at Mr. Badass over here.

I said to the officer, "Public Intoxication would mean that she is a danger to herself or others. This girl couldn't harm a fly. There is no need to handcuff her."

The officer bowed up to me even though he was five inches shorter than I was.

He yelled, "Do you want to be handcuffed too, asshole?"

A few of my friends pulled me away from the officer to make sure I didn't say something stupid. The officer then spoke to his partner. While they were talking they pulled out a Penal Code book.

What a bunch of fucking amateurs.

The officers decided to take the handcuffs off Gretchen who had been crying the whole time. She appeared to look somewhat relieved after the cuffs were off.

The officer charged Gretchen with a Minor in Possession which meant that she was not going to be arrested or taken to jail. The charge was only a Class C Misdemeanor, which was the same category as a simple traffic ticket. A Public Intoxication charge would have been much worse on her record.

Gretchen was still pretty upset and pretty drunk. I told her I would take her home, and we would relax for the rest of the day.

On the car ride home, Gretchen began to sob uncontrollably.

She cried, "I will never be able to become a teacher because of this."

I replied, "It's going to be ok. We can fix this."

I explained to her that this charge could easily be dismissed and that I would do everything I could to help her.

She snapped at me and said, "You don't know what the hell you are talking about. I'm fucked!"

I exclaimed, "Yeah, sure, I don't know what I am talking about. I majored in criminal justice and I'm a certified police officer. What the hell do I know, right?"

"Well I know one thing. This is all your fault."

Of course.

Gretchen began to psychotically explain to me that since I was the one to drive them to Sonic and buy them drinks it was inevitably my fault that she was charged with an M.I.P.

Whenever Gretchen knew she was immensely wrong, she automatically shifted the blame on someone other than herself.

Once we got back home, she started to scream because she was so angry.

She kept yelling, "It's all your fault. No one will ever hire me because of you."

There are many reasons why a company would not want to hire someone like you, Gretchen.

I explained, "I will go to court with you and help you with this but you cannot put the blame on me. You need to watch what you say. I could easily leave you and let you deal with this shit yourself. I have no problem with that."

Gretchen quickly became silent. She softly said, "I'm sorry for what I said. It's my fault and I didn't mean to blame you."

I'm a forgiving person but how many chances do you give someone before pulling the plug?

Gretchen felt so bad about everything, so she ordered a pizza and cinnamon sticks from Dominoes.

I will never turn down food, and pizza is the key to my heart.

Gretchen said, "I hope these slices of pepperoni will help you forgive me."

Shut up and pass me the ranch woman.

That night, I called my good friend Casey who had been practicing law for about three years. I told him the entire story and he agreed to represent Gretchen in court.

I said, "Casey will help you get this charge erased forever."

She replied, "Thank you so much! I don't know what I would do without you, Juddy."

A month later, Gretchen had her court date. As promised, I was present along with my friend Casey. He got the M.I.P. charge not only dismissed but also completely expunged off Gretchen's record.

After court was adjourned, we all walked outside to head home. I told Gretchen to go wait in the car while I talked to Casey.

I thanked him multiple times, and paid him an undisclosed amount of money. He gave me a pretty good discount which helped big time. Gretchen had no idea about the payment to Casey. I have never been one to boast about what I do for someone. All I knew was that I did the right thing.

On the way home, Gretchen said, "You have no idea how much you helped me today. Thank you for being by my side and helping me through this. I love you, Juddy."

We tried our best to forget about the entire thing and move forward. I was just glad that her future career in teaching was no longer in jeopardy.

Right around the corner was the day that all guys look forward to every year. It was the one holiday where women wear jaw-dropping outfits that barely covered their skin.

God bless the holiday of Halloween.

It still amazes me that women get angry if guys stare at them while their cleavage is popping out like bulging watermelons while their butt cheeks are glistening in the moonlight.

Most of the time with costumes, people are pretending to be something they're not. In Gretchen's case, she was actively portraying her drunken alter ego, which I hadn't seen in a long time. She dressed up as a she-devil with red horns, a tail, and high heels.

I dressed up as Jeff Spicoli (Sean Penn) from 'Fast Times and Ridgemont High.'

We started to tip back shots as fast as the bartenders could make them. Jaeger Bombs, Vegas Bombs, and Kamikazes were being funneled one by one. We were drunk in a matter of minutes.

There was a girl at the party that night that I had taken as a date to a fraternity event about a year before I met Gretchen. Her name was Stacey. She and I never did anything physically intimate. We were just good friends.

Not only did the presence of Stacey put Gretchen in a bad mood, but she happened to be dressed up in the exact she-devil costume as Gretchen.

Just my fucking luck.

As soon as Gretchen saw Stacey at the party the psycho switch was immediately thrown into the 'ON' position. Gretchen ran up to me and said, "Do you think Stacey looks better than me? If you do then we are done."

I said, "Of course not you look way better than her."

"You're lying. I know you're lying. Why don't you just go have sex with her tonight if that would make you happy."

Sex with Stacey would have probably been quite delightful, but I'm not a cheater.

About a dozen shots later, Gretchen had once again morphed into the gremlin and I was doomed. The remainder of the party I was attempting to calm the wicked beast. No matter what I did she was infuriated at absolutely everything.

She kept saying, "Let me party with my friends. Leave me alone! Go hang out with Stacey the slut!"

She was bouncing from one side of the bar to the other consuming shots at every turn. I tried to have a good time with some of my buddies but I just wanted to leave.

I somehow convinced Gretchen to leave the Halloween party early. Maybe I could at least put a lid on her shit so she could let it all out at home and not in the public eye.

Naturally, like every drunken individual on this earth at two in the morning Gretchen was craving Whataburger; as was I.

Once we arrived at the drive thru Gretchen proceeded to order.

She slowly spewed out, "Yeah, um yeah. I want to get like a dozen bacon taquitos with super extra picante sauce and a cheeseburger."

I wanted to throw up. Knowing that Gretchen would be stuffing her face full of a meal that could feed a family of four made me sick. Maybe the greasy food would absorb the large amount of alcohol that had flooded her stomach. That would hopefully reduce the aggression that she was releasing at an alarming rate.

On the ride home, she crammed about half of the taquitos and the entire cheeseburger in her mouth. I could smell the saturated fat on her breath.

We pulled up to Gretchen's townhome after a short drive. As we walked in the door a chill ran down my spine. The anticipation of what might transpire in that haunted house had me on the edge. I slowly walked into Gretchen's room otherwise known at the 'torture chamber.'

Immediately when I shut the door, Gretchen began to glare at me in a way that made me cringe in fear. Then all a sudden I saw what looked like blood coming from the sides of her mouth but then quickly realized it was only picante sauce.

As Gretchen was ferociously staring at me, she began to make this grunting sound. It could best be described as an extremely constipated grizzly bear.

Maybe she just needed to take a dump?

A violent tirade of epic proportions began to unfold. Gretchen charged at me and began to slap me and hit me in the chest. The demonic things that were coming out of her mouth were hard to understand. The majority of it included fowl language and rude remarks directed at Stacey.

How do I stop this violent monster?

An idea came to mind.

What if I joined her and talked shit about Stacey while feeding her more taquitos? Negative verbal communication with positive reinforcement should do the trick.

I said, "Yeah, Stacey, is such a slut. You looked so much better than her tonight. You were the hottest she-devil ever! Would you like another taquito, honey?"

Gretchen said, "Yeah, Stacey sucks, and of course I want another taquito!"

After destroying what was left in the doggie bag, Gretchen finally came back to reality and started to cry.

Not this shit again.

She cried out, "I hate all this drama and I don't mean to blame you. I'm just insecure around the girls of your past."

Finally a shred of honesty.

I said, "I love you and only you. That's all that matters."

We both decided to call a truce and get into bed. There was an awkward moment of silence. I didn't know if it was kosher to initiate a sexual encounter. I wanted to let her know that I was drawn to her and nobody else. I grabbed her pulled her over to me and began to passionately glaze her greasy lips.

Halfway through the sexual journey, I noticed that Gretchen not only still had picante sauce on the right corner of her mouth, but she also had a piece of bacon stuck in her teeth. I kept going but it was like having sex with a breakfast burrito.

The next morning, I knew I had to have a very serious talk with Gretchen. For the first time, she had finally opened up and told me about her insecurity. Although I empathized with her grief, there was no way I could let her behavior be tolerated anymore.

"Gretchen the way you treat me when you're drunk is unacceptable and humiliating. How would you like it if I treated you that way?" I said.

Gretchen sadly replied, "I would hate it. I can't help that I'm insecure, that is just the way I am. I'm not confident in myself, and I consider the girls of your past a serious threat to me."

"Have I ever been unfaithful to you or lied to you?"

"No, and I know you would never hurt me. I just don't trust them."

"You have directed your anger at me, and I don't deserve it."

"I know I have a problem, and I am doing my best to fix it. I love you so much, and I want to be with you."

"Gretchen I have given you so many chances to change, and I know deep down you love me, but if anything like this happens again I have to say goodbye."

Gretchen began to cry. She grabbed me and held me close.

She sobbed, "I love you, Juddy. I promise that this will never happen again. I will never bring up your exes or get angry with you. You're right. You don't deserve this. You deserve much better."

This was the first time that Gretchen admitted that she had a problem. It looked like there was hope and that she wanted to be a better companion to me. Even though there were rough times, I really did love this woman. I was committed to the relationship, but at the same time I was confused.

Is this how all relationships are? Am I the only one going through this shit? Would I be better off alone?

Maybe I needed to take Gretchen out of the drama filled world that she lived in; go some place where we wouldn't run into any of my exes. Some of our best moments were when we were alone.

I wanted to take us on a vacation, and I decided to book us a cruise. Since I had a steady paycheck, I had been saving up money for a while. I felt that if I did something special to show her how much I cared for her, she would bury the evil gremlin forever.

Maybe an all-inclusive alcoholic cruise wasn't necessarily the smartest choice, but at least she would be free from the drama. I was hoping to spend time alone with her and far away from everything. I figured that if I could pull her away from the people that provoked her anger she would comprehend that the love that we had for each other was very special.

What if I'm the one that provokes her anger?

About a month later, we sailed off into the sunset and embarked on a five-day cruise. We were always on the top deck by sunrise to claim our rightful spots by the pool. After getting hammered for about four hours, we would stumble over to the buffet where we loaded our plates up with a shitload of food. Gretchen especially enjoyed the breakfast tacos.

No surprise there.

I had booked two excursions. One was jet skiing and the other was parasailing. The parasailing was probably the best part of the trip. We were flying high and gazing at the beautiful scenery in the Caribbean. It was worth every penny.

One night, we attended an acrobatic dance show on the ship after dinner. It was a very entertaining show and it looked like Gretchen was really enjoying herself. We then walked up to the top deck and marveled at the stars. Next to us was a couple about our age.

Suddenly, the guy got on one knee and proposed to his girlfriend. The small amount of people up there all began to clap and cheer. Gretchen had a big smile on her face.

She asked, "You think that will ever be us?"

I said, "Maybe one day."

I pulled her close to me and gave her a kiss. It was almost like we were a normal couple again. We both got trashed the rest of the trip but there was no sign of the gremlin. The vacation may have led to the destruction of the monster that lied within Gretchen. It was the miracle that I had been praying for. Maybe it was time to finally move in a positive direction with our relationship, which we had been building for nearly two years.

When we got back from the cruise it was towards the end of November. Gretchen had only about two weeks left in school before she went on winter break. I was already contemplating gift ideas for Christmas and found the perfect one. I bought Gretchen an all-in-one day spa package. It included a Swedish massage, manicure, pedicure, and hot stone therapy. If that gift didn't get me a little action underneath the mistletoe, then I would just give up.

We were going to be apart for Christmas so we decided to exchange gifts early.

Gretchen opened her card.

She exclaimed, "Oh, thank you so much. This is the best Christmas gift I have ever gotten. My gift for you isn't that great."

I told her, "Whatever you got me I'm sure it is amazing."

I opened my gift, and it was a cologne set. It looked like a knock-off brand from Wal-Mart, but I didn't say a word. It was called 'Night Hawk.' I opened the bottle of cologne and sprayed it on my wrist. It was one of the worst scents I had ever encountered. It was a horrid sour smell. The odor was like a used gym sock soaked in cat piss. I began to cough and sneeze uncontrollably.

Gretchen asked, "Do you like it?"

I replied, "Yes I do. I just think I put too much on. It's quite pungent which is a good thing."

It took everything I had not to blow chunks. The smell was seeping into my throat, and it wasn't going away. With my bloodshot eyes, I looked at Gretchen in the face and said, "Thank you, honey for the wonderful gift. Merry Christmas!"

About a week before school let out for the holiday break, Gretchen's sorority put on a Christmas pajama party. I was stoked about it because I have always enjoyed dressing like a moron and getting hammered with friends.

I had on a Santa hat, short shorts, red knee-high stockings, and slippers. Gretchen had on pajama pants and a T-shirt on with a Santa hat. We were ready to suck down some eggnog and whiskey.

I was tipsy pretty fast, so I went out on the dance floor by myself to bust some moves.

I don't know how to dance, but I do know how to make people laugh by looking like an idiot.

People slowly began to migrate towards the dance floor, except for Gretchen. She was busy talking in the corner to a guy named Kyle who happened to be a new member of the same fraternity I was in. I didn't know Kyle very well, so I went up to introduce myself.

I said, "Hey, man. I'm, Juddy, Gretchen's boyfriend."

He replied, "Yeah, I've heard a lot about you. Nice to meet you, man."

Gretchen just gave me this puzzled looked in the background.

I asked, "Gretchen do you want a drink?"

"Yeah! Thanks, Juddy," she said.

I bought all three of us a few drinks at the bar because 'tis the season to be jolly.'

There was a strange feeling in the air though. I have felt it before.

The way Gretchen and Kyle were conversing to each other in the corner was odd. There were some flirtatious mannerisms that were definitely present. Every time I would come up to Gretchen, she would give me this perturbed look as if I was interrupting something. Of course that spawned an argument between us.

Towards the end of the night, I went up to Gretchen and said, "We are leaving. Let's go. I'm tired."

She complained, "There is an after party I want to go to."

"Not happening. We are going home."

When we arrived home I brought Gretchen into her room.

She whined, "Why did we have to go home early?"

I said, "We are going to need a good night sleep tonight. I got us tickets to the 'Christmas Carol' play at the theatre downtown as a surprise!"

"Oh that is so sweet of you, but I have to study for finals all day tomorrow. I'm sorry, Juddy. I can't go."

"Can you study during the day and come with me to the show that night?"

"I have four finals on Monday, and I'm so far behind. I'm sorry. Is there anyone that can take my ticket and go with you?"

"I guess I can find someone to go with me at the VERY LAST MINUTE."

Gretchen didn't pick up on the sarcasm.

There was no one I really had in mind besides her, my girlfriend. The next morning, I headed out so that Gretchen could start studying. I tried to think of people to invite to the play.

A theatrical Christmas 'Bro-Date' was simply out of the question. My parents were out of town for the weekend, so I couldn't ask my mother.

I didn't want the tickets to go to waste, so I decided to go by myself. It felt refreshing to have some time alone, but Gretchen was on my mind the whole time.

Was she lying to me about studying?

The play was absolutely incredible, and all the actors did a wonderful job. Afterwards, I called Gretchen to see how her studying was going but she didn't answer. It was a long, quiet ride home that night, but for some reason…I enjoyed it.

A few days later, I was planning on driving up to see Gretchen for the weekend. It was the last time I would see her before we both went home for the Christmas break.

I knew Gretchen was busy with her final exams, so I tried not to bother her too much. I had already packed my bag in advance and was going to leave straight from work.

Once the work day was over I sent her a text that read, "Leaving work now. Be there in an hour. Can't wait to see you!"

There was no response.

About halfway there I received a call from her.

Gretchen said, "Juddy, I need to talk to you about something."

I replied, "Ok well I'll be there in thirty minutes so we can just talk then."

"No we need to talk now. This relationship isn't working out and I want to break up."

My heart sank deep into my chest. I pulled over into the nearest gas station.

I pleaded, "What did I do wrong? I thought we loved each other? I have been trying so hard to make you happy, Gretchen."

She revealed, "I'm just not in love with you anymore."

"When did you stop loving me?"

"A very long time ago."

It felt like she had just pierced a sword right into my beating heart.

I pleaded, "All those times that you told me you loved me and all the memories we have together? They mean nothing to you?"

She replied, "I was forcing it to happen and it never felt natural. Good bye, Juddy."

My world, once again, came crashing down and I began to cry.

She hung up before I could say anything more. I was completely broken and fucking pissed. I quickly turned around and headed straight home. Once I got to my apartment, I went into my room and locked the door. I was trying to hold myself together while tears shot down my face. I kept asking myself, "What did I do wrong?"

The pain was consuming me quickly. I didn't want to speak to anyone. I just wanted to be alone. I got back in my car and drove to a nearby bar. It was one my favorite places to go back home. It was a small pub and nothing fancy which was right up my alley.

I took a seat and ordered a glass of whiskey. It never tasted as good as it did right then. I had a few sips and just sat there contemplating everything. The more sips I took, the more depressed I started to become. As my vision became more impaired, the memories I had of Gretchen began to fizzle away.

After about two hours, I was about to head home. I was pretty drunk, so I was going to do the honorable thing and call my mom for a ride home. I looked at my phone which I had put on silent, and I had five missed calls from a very good friend of mine named Matt. I really didn't feel like talking to anyone, but I had a strange feeling that I should call him back.

Matt was a close friend of mine, and if he was calling me over and over, it had to be important. The last time he called this many times, he was looking for the nearest Planned Parenthood.

We had known each other for a few years now. We were also members of the same fraternity. He was still in college, like Gretchen and, he was also well connected to the massive web of drama that consumed the lives of many people. I called him back, and he answered.

He asked, "Hey, man. Where are you?"

I replied, "At a small pub back home about to head out."

"Go back in, take a seat, and get another drink."

I sat back down at the bar, and ordered another glass of whiskey.

Matt explained, "This is going to hurt, but I have to tell you what has been going on behind your back. I am only doing this because I know you would do the same for me."

He began to divulge that Gretchen had been having sex with Kyle, the guy from the Christmas party, for the past three weeks. Each time Gretchen would claim to have 'study sessions,' the two of them would explore each other's private parts extensively.

To think that I was friendly to this asshole and bought him drinks just made me want to vomit. Even though Gretchen and I had already broken up, this revelation sent me over the edge.

I called my mom to pick me up. When she arrived, I drunkenly stumbled into the car and cried the whole way home. She didn't ask me what happened. I think she already knew.

When I got home, I went inside and locked myself in my room. For the next few days, I lived a life of solitude. The only time I came out of my room was to dispose of any human waste or gather food.

I started to destroy everything that reminded me of her. I thought I would heal after a while, but the pain was engulfing my life and taking control of my mind. I didn't want to let the sadness win. I wanted to prevail and survive the deplorable nightmare.

Gretchen had literally sucked the living soul out of my body. I felt less human and more like a robot without feelings or emotions. I became numb to love for a while and nothing was blocking my inner depression that had been growing with every breakup.

I went on a dating hiatus for a while. I didn't want to be alone forever. I just wanted to be happy.

Gretchen had turned my world into a dark cold place filled with depression and psychotic nightmares. My emotional strength was ceasing to exist, and I was finding it hard to grasp onto hope anymore.

Relationship Report:

Pros	Cons
• Loving • Not a Blabbermouth • Encouraging • Good appetite • Great smile	• Reality Manipulator • Cheater • Violent • Multiple Identities • Blame-Shifter

Total Time Lost	2 years
Hours of Unpaid Labor	250
Cheated?	Yes
Emotional Trauma (On a Scale of 1 to 10)	10
Sex Life	Below Average
Physical Abuse	Yes

Total Montary Loses: $11,560.00

- Dinner Dates: 4x per month @ $60 per date
- Special Occasion Dates: 1x every 6 months @ $150.00 per date
- Gifts (Holidays and Anniversaries): 6x per year @ $100.00 per gift
- Vacation Cruise & Lawyer Fee: $4,000.00

Chapter 10-Carlisle 'The Virtual Girlfriend'

After several months of being alone, I was sucked in to the dating world yet again. I wanted to give up, but I knew I had to be strong in order to survive the emotionally broken world I lived in. I kept marching on, but the future was so unclear.

Blind dates are a gamble, but I was willing to try anything at this point. Two friends of mine decided to organize a double date. I had never been on one of these, and I had no idea what my date was going to look like.

Knowing my luck it will probably be a ghastly swamp creature of some sort.

I arrived early and sat in the lobby of the Mexican restaurant we were all meeting at. All of a sudden, a drop dead gorgeous blonde walked in the door. She was tall with long curly hair, brown eyes, and radiant skin.

Yeah right. I wish.

Following right behind the blonde were my friends, Paul and Lindsay.

Lindsay looked at me and said, "Juddy, this is my friend, Carlisle, and she is your blind date."

My jaw dropped to the ground, and I had to make sure there wasn't any drool coming out of my mouth. In a shaky voice, I said, "Hello, Carlisle, I'm…Juddy."

"Hello there. Nice to meet you," she said.

We all sat down in a booth and ordered some drinks. Carlisle and I were getting along extremely well once we started to get to know each other. She had a great sense of humor, and she seemed very kind hearted.

That's how it always starts…

Carlisle said, "Lindsay showed me a picture of you last night. You had a tuxedo on with a bow tie. You looked quite handsome."

I said, "Thank you but I assure you the pleasure is all mine."

Upon finishing dinner, Carlisle asked, "Do you want to split the bill?"

I responded, "Of course not. It's my treat. Thank you for not bailing on me."

"I never flake on my friends."

I couldn't believe she had offered to help pay for dinner. This told me that she was most likely independent, a quality that was always hard to find in my experience.

We all migrated to a nearby bar afterwards. Carlisle was a big fan of small pubs, rather than big fancy nightclubs.

"I hate nightclubs. It's too crowded and too expensive," she said.

I think I might ask her to marry me.

At the pub, Carlisle and I began to flirt with each other quite a bit. The more drinks I had, the more times I found myself kissing her on the cheek. I may have been too aggressive, but she seemed to enjoy it.

Carlisle was a lot of fun to be around and even bought a couple of rounds for the four of us. We had drinks for about three hours, and we were all pretty hammered. Lindsay invited all of us back to her apartment for more drinks.

Once we arrived at Lindsay's place, we all took a few shots, and had a couple beers. Everyone was in good spirits, and it was already about 2am.

Lindsay and Paul left the room to go get frisky. Carlisle and I sat on the couch and put on a movie. We started to kiss for a bit, and then our horniness kicked into overdrive. We both looked at each other as if we were the last couple on earth, and we had to immediately repopulate the human race. There were no words spoken and before the opening scene of the movie, our clothes were off.

Normally if I'm drunk and nude on a couch it's because of a frat party gone wrong. This time I was with a girl, which was a much better change of scenery.

The sex was highly aggressive. There was scratching, biting, and even pinching. She was a ferocious animal, and I tried my best to keep up.

It had been awhile since I had mated with a female, so my potency was in dire jeopardy. I was deathly afraid that that my response time would be much quicker than usual. Luckily, the whiskey inside helped me go the extra mile. I was able to finish the fight in an adequate amount of time.

Carlisle said, "Wow. That is the first time I have ever slept with someone on the first date."

I replied, "You might think I'm lying but I'm in the same boat."

"It was totally worth it and I have no regrets."

"Likewise."

The next morning, we all woke up and had breakfast. All four of us were smiling from ear to ear.

Looks like everyone got lucky last night.

Carlisle and I had a moment alone before we headed back home.

I said, "I know we just slept together, and this may be just a formality, but I would like to take you out on another date. That is of course if you would like to."

Carlisle chuckled, "Well you have already sealed the deal but you do owe me dinner."

We laughed, exchanged numbers, and headed home.

The following week, I took her out to PF Changs. We feasted like a king and queen. Our dinner consisted of lettuce wraps, spicy chicken, shrimp fried rice, and sake. We then finished the meal off with one slice of 'the great wall of chocolate.' It was a piece of chocolate mousse cake that was the size of my head, and it was drizzled with raspberry sauce.

We got to know a lot more about each other at the dinner table that night. We both loved scary movies, heavy metal, and all types of food.

She invited me over to her place afterwards. When we pulled up, I was surprised to see that Carlisle had her own two-story house. It appeared that she did pretty well for herself.

We walked into the kitchen to make drinks. I looked over at the fridge and saw multiple pictures of Carlisle and some dude.

I immediately stopped and asked, "Are you involved with someone else?"

Carlisle freaked out and exclaimed, "No! He's my ex. We broke up about three months ago. You have nothing to worry about."

She proceeded to take down every picture of him in the house and throw it in the garbage.

I wonder what happened between them?

We went upstairs to her bedroom and once again aggressively stripped each other's clothes off as we did a week before on the couch. It was a much more comfortable environment on the king-sized bed she had. There was only one abnormal aspect that evening. While we were rocking the bed frame, I happened to notice a large framed picture that was wall mounted above the headpiece of the bed. It was Carlisle and her ex-boyfriend. It was one of the most awkward moments of my life.

This poor bastard on the wall is watching me bone his ex-girlfriend. All I could do was say, "Sorry, bro. My bad."

Even though Carlisle eventually took the picture down, I could always feel his angry eyes staring at us in the bedroom.

About two weeks into our relationship, I started to become curious as to what Carlisle did for a living. I was surfing the net one day and was perusing one of my favorite websites Break.com. The website featured all different types of funny videos, pictures, and articles.

On Break, there was this video titled, 'Off-Roading with Sexy Crystal.' From the look of the image, the girl looked identical to Carlisle. I clicked on the video and there she was.

Carlisle was riding in an off road vehicle with a white low cut shirt on. Her larger than average boobs were ferociously bouncing up and down while riding through the rough terrain. In the description of the video, I happened to notice an Internet ad. It read, "Do you want to see this babe topless? CLICK HERE NOW!"

The ad had a picture of Carlisle on it clear as day. In the picture, she was wearing glasses, a black bra, and a black tie.

Oh man what the hell have I got myself into now?

Like a lot of the lonely men around the world, I clicked on the ad. I was redirected to Carlisle's main website which had a video of her making out with another chick wearing nothing but lingerie. There were also pictures everywhere of Carlisle topless plastered all over the site.

I wonder if my mother would approve?

Carlisle was apparently a 'cam-girl,' which was known in the adult industry as a virtual girlfriend. She went online randomly throughout the week mostly at night. She would either strip or pleasure herself in front of a webcam for money. It all depended on how much cash the customers wanted to piss away. These sexual acts could be viewed by many individuals at once or privately with a one-on-one chat for a ridiculous amount of money. Carlisle never saw her customers face to face, but they saw her complete anatomy from top to bottom.

Instantaneously, I had a bad taste in my mouth. I didn't know how to react. Was I lucky because I am dating a girl that most guys would pay big money just to see naked?

Needless to say, I was conflicted.

The next day, I went over to Carlisle's house for dinner. I confronted her about what I had discovered.

I said, "I saw one of your business ads online last night. They call you 'Sexy Crystal' right?"

Carlisle's face turned bright red. She was silent and looked extremely embarrassed. This was quite ironic coming from a girl who obviously doesn't seem too shy on the Internet with strangers.

Carlisle replied, "I won't be mad if you want to leave. I understand how this must make you feel."

We both had a long talk about everything. She began to fill me in on rise to Internet stardom. She was a Playboy Playmate at the age of eighteen. She took the money she made from that gig and started up her own website. She had been doing 'web-shows' for about five years. She also had a pretty large customer clientele. She had customers that lived all over the world including: Europe, Japan, and Australia.

I didn't want to pass any judgment on her but it's hard when the girl you are dating is 'finger-blasting' herself on a webcam every other night.

I said to her, "I respect you for being independent. I'm not going to lie. Your profession creeps me out just a bit but I enjoy being with you.

Carlisle smiled, and I decided to proceed as planned and take the relationship step by step.

About a month into our relationship, I could tell that Carlisle was working hard to make me a happy man. She would make home cooked meals for me all the time, which was huge in my book. She also sometimes paid for a night out on the town. Whether it was dinner and a movie or some fun activity like going to a museum, we always had a lot of fun together. She took care of me, which was something I was not use to whatsoever.

In the bedroom, Carlisle was wild and crazy often putting on random sexy outfits to seduce me. She would walk in the room with eight-inch heels and a corset, and I was mesmerized.

Honestly to seduce any guy a girl really just needs to take her clothes off. On the other hand if a guy randomly takes his clothes off in front of a girl, she calls the police.

Sometimes, I felt like one of her sorry ass customers. Although, in the end, I wasn't the one behind a computer screen yanking my wiener and shelling out money.

I felt like I was living in a dream. Things couldn't have been better. Unfortunately, things can sometimes be too good to be true.

After we had been dating for about six months, Carlisle's ex-boyfriend began to call her on a regular basis. His name was Rick.

Carlisle and Rick had dated for about five years. They began seeing each other back in high school. Rick not only cheated on Carlisle, but he also sucked the money from her wallet as well. He was unemployed for a long time, so Carlisle paid for all of his bills and even bought him a brand new Tahoe, which he still had.

Every time Rick called while I was around Carlisle kept telling me, "You have nothing to worry about. I want to be with you."

She kept claiming that her and Rick were history but I was skeptical.

A couple of weeks went by, and Carlisle began to be flaky with me. She wouldn't return my calls at times and she would always make excuses not to see me. She would always say she had to work late.

Then one evening, Carlisle asked me to have dinner at her house. She made me my favorite meal. It was chicken fried steak, garlic mashed potatoes, and bacon wrapped asparagus. I was in heaven, but I felt she was either buttering me up for pleasure or preparing to inflict me with pain.

After we finished dinner and a few glasses of wine, we went upstairs to the game room to watch a movie. Once we sat down, Carlisle said, "Juddy, I have to tell you something. I need to be honest with you."

Those words are typically followed by a sharp twist of the knife.

She explained, "I have been sleeping with Rick for the past two weeks, and I think we might end up getting back together."

I sarcastically chuckled, "Wow. That's just fucking great isn't it?"

"I'm really sorry. You just caught me at a strange time in my life."

"Obviously, there is no reason for me to stay. I thought we had something special going. I guess I was wrong. Hope that broke piece of shit makes you happy. Good luck with that."

I got up and stormed out the front door. As soon as I started my car, Carlisle came running out onto the driveway with tears in her eyes. She didn't say anything. She just gazed at me while I drove off.

Later that night, she sent me a barrage of text messages and even called a few times. I ignored every single one of them. There was nothing to be said and after a few days…she was gone.

Our relationship had suddenly disappeared.

The bad luck with women was continuing to follow me like a plague. Failure after failure, my heart had become weaker. I didn't know how much of this shit I could handle without losing control. I kept myself together as best as I could, but everyone on this earth has a breaking point, and I was getting extremely close to it.

Chapter 11-Aberdeen 'The Double Crossing Ice Dancer'

About three months later, a good friend of mine named Jessica decided to introduce me to one of her best girlfriends one day. She was an ice dancer for a Pro Hockey team and a recent college graduate. Her name was Aberdeen.

We all went downtown one night for drinks. It was Jessica, Aberdeen, and about six of our friends. Aberdeen was quite unique from any girl I had ever met. She had an exotic look to her with dark hair, sharp brown eyes, and naturally tan skin. The deep brown shade of her eyes was her most captivating attribute.

I said, "Hello, I'm, Juddy. I have heard a lot of good things about you!"

Aberdeen replied, "Same here. It's nice to meet you."

Even though she seemed nice upon arrival I could tell that she was a girl that always got what she wanted. Wherever she wanted to go around town that's where we went. No one else really had a say in the matter. We bar hopped several times to various locations around the city. I paid for every drink she had, and she really didn't seem to appreciate the gesture all that much. It was almost like that was just expected and mandatory.

A simple 'Thank You' would have sufficed.

During that particular evening, I was well guarded of the signals I gave her. I didn't know if I even liked her yet, but I was trying to feel her out first. I didn't want to insinuate that I was like every other guy that probably hit on her on a regular basis. I played it cool the whole night. I didn't try any flirtatious moves and basically acted like I didn't give a shit.

I am beginning to like this approach.

Towards the end of the night, Aberdeen asked, "Why haven't you asked for my number yet?"

I calmly replied, "I'm right next to you. Why do I need your number?"

Aberdeen looked at me with a baffled look.

Rejected.

She quickly started to walk off and I grabbed her hand.

I chuckled, "I was only kidding. May I have your number? I would like to take you to brunch tomorrow if you're free."

She answered, "Absolutely! I love would love that!"

The next day, Aberdeen and I went out for brunch at a nearby patio pub before I went back home. Maybe if it was just the two of us, I could get to know the real Aberdeen. I may have been passing judgment on her too quickly.

As soon as we walked into the pub for brunch, every single guy in the place began to eyeball her. Even the guys with girls at their table were breaking their necks to catch a glimpse.

We sat down and ordered some bottomless mimosas, which was one of the best drink specials known to man. As we were indulging in our hangover meal, I asked, "What do you do besides performing as an ice dancer?"

She replied, "I have been modeling since was eighteen."

I think I still had horrendous amounts of pimples at that age. Plus, I don't think my highlighted bangs and braces would've gone over well with Calvin Klein.

I have always viewed models as self-centered, pretentious, and snobby individuals. Hopefully, this wasn't the case with Aberdeen, but again, I was still on the defensive side of things.

During our conversation, she began to open up to me about her trouble with guys. Aberdeen seemed to always go after the assholes.

Sounds oddly familiar.

She explained, "Dating those guys made me a little bit of a bitch, and I don't want you to get the wrong impression of me."

I replied, "I don't think you're a bitch at all. I believe that you might be hiding who you really are. You seem very kind hearted on the inside."

"I'm trying hard to be better these days. You are a very nice guy, and I have enjoyed meeting you."

"Thank you for joining me today, Aberdeen."

It was strange delving into a deep emotional conversation so fast, but I felt comfortable around her. After we had brunch, we hugged each other goodbye, and I asked her if she wanted to go to dinner with me next weekend.

She said, "Yes, of course! I'd love to!"

During the days following up to our next rendezvous, we called and texted each other quite a bit. Like me, she was quite humorous. She would always send me jokes and funny pictures that she found on the Internet to brighten my day. It appeared that we were quite compatible.

Although something told me that in order to date a woman like this, I was going to need a lot of money.

Better start selling drugs.

That following weekend, I took Aberdeen to a nice sushi place. We sat at the bar and ordered a wide array of exotic rolls. Aberdeen had a good appetite on her. She kept up with me roll after roll. She never hesitated and helped me consume at least five-dozen of them. It was a damn good meal, and we both had soy sauce dripping from our lips.

Aberdeen said, "I don't think I've ever eaten that much in my entire life. I'm kind of embarrassed."

I chuckled, "Don't be. I am kind of impressed. Nice work!"

We sunk down a couple sake bombs and headed out.

I drove Aberdeen back to her apartment which wasn't too far away. Once we parked, I got out to open the door for her. As soon as she got out, she grabbed my shirt, and yanked me towards her. We locked lips, and started to make out for the first time. It tasted like seaweed but I didn't mind. I wasn't going to invite myself in to her apartment, because I always felt that to be lame. Instead, I put the ball in her court.

I asked, "Do you need me to walk you to the door?"

She laughed, "No that's ok. It's just a few feet away."

She lived on the first story and we were right next to her apartment.

Smooth move dipshit.

I said, "I had a really great time, Aberdeen. Thank You."

She replied, "Yeah, I enjoyed it. Thank you for the all those sushi rolls. I think I will now take a long nap."

It was a successful date.

So far things appeared to be running smoothly. I was enjoying my time with her, but quite possibly, this was just the calm before the storm.

A good friend of mine was getting married in a month, and all my buddies were bringing dates, except for yours truly. I decided to take a chance and invite Aberdeen as my date.

I called her up and asked, "I hope this is not too forward, but would you be my date to the wedding?"

She exclaimed, "Yes, I'd love to go! I love weddings!

A few weeks later, Aberdeen and I headed to the wedding which was about an hour outside of town. She was wearing a black cocktail dress with heels and had her hair up. She looked quite amazing, and I was excited to have her as my date.

After the wedding ceremony was over. I began to introduce her to everyone. Aberdeen fit right in.

"All of your friends are so nice! I'm having a great time!" she said.

I replied, "I'm so glad you came with me. Thank You, Aberdeen"

Since Aberdeen was an ice dancer, she was dominating the dance floor. I couldn't keep up with her moves. She was all over the place and looked like a professional. I had a lot of guys come up to me complimenting me on her. Some of them even got in trouble for starring at Aberdeen's silicone chest units. Those puppies were installed when Aberdeen was nineteen-years-old, which seemed to be one hell of a high school graduation gift.

I had reserved a hotel room for Aberdeen and I, so we didn't have to drive anywhere. After the reception was over, we headed back to our room. I wasn't expecting anything physically intimate to happen but the large amount of alcohol in our stomachs inevitably put us in the mood for some sexual exploration.

As soon as we got in bed together, there was a silent awkward moment where neither individual knew the sexual boundaries of the other.

The guy is reluctant to make a move due to the fear of rejection and looking like a pervert. The girl is reluctant to make a move due to the fear of looking like a slut. Life is too short to worry about such things.

I grabbed her, wrapped my arms around her, and began to play some tonsil hockey.

There was a slight problem with the kissing situation. Making out with Aberdeen was like kissing a chipmunk. It almost felt like she was gnawing on a piece of corn. I didn't even have time to get my tongue inside. Every time I tried to get near the back of her throat, she would close her teeth and try to chew on my lips.

I'm not trying to say that I'm the best kisser, but I guess was just deathly afraid of what she might do to other parts of my body.

I then proceeded to the lower region of her dark skinned body with my hand. I was down inside her cave for quite some time. After a while, I was beginning to feel the early stages of carpel tunnel syndrome.

She didn't make any moves underneath my gym shorts but that didn't bother me at all.

Before my wrist broke, I decided to call it a night.

All in all, I would say that it was a pretty successful weekend. The only downside was that I couldn't strum a guitar for a week.

About two weeks after the wedding, I invited Aberdeen out so she could meet some of my close friends. Among some of them were my pals Will and Ashley, who happened to be proud new owners of a fitness facility. We were all going out to celebrate their success with a grand opening party at a bar downtown.

To be polite, at the beginning of the party, I introduced Aberdeen to Will and Ashley. I was curious about the new gym and asked Will, "How much would a membership cost at your place?"

Will replied, "It's $150 a month for unlimited workouts, a personal coach, and diet education."

Aberdeen immediately interjected and blurted out, "$150 bucks? That's such a rip off! My family has a personal trainer who trains all of us for $100 a month."

I was disgusted and embarrassed. I quickly stopped her mid-sentence and said, "Aberdeen, they built their gym from the ground up using their own money and a lot of hard work. We are here tonight to celebrate their success. Why would you say something like that?"

She gazed at me like I had said something wrong.

The irony.

I guess she truly believed that there was nothing wrong with saying such an insulting comment. I took Will aside and apologized for Aberdeen's rude remark. He really didn't seem to mind, but to me it was completely disrespectful.

I went back to Aberdeen and said, "Do you know how much hard work they put into their gym?"

She shot back, "You're overreacting. You need to chill out."

There's nothing more infuriating than someone telling me to chill out.

I told her, "I guess no one ever taught you to think before you speak."

She childishly replied, "I'm sorry, Dad."

"Wow. Unreal."

The private event ended, and Aberdeen still wanted to party out on the town but I was over it. It's not her money that was getting thrown around, so I guess she really didn't give a shit.

I said, "We are calling it a night."

She began to pout like a child. I had reserved a hotel room for the night downtown, and I was ready to go to bed. The whole way back to the hotel in the cab, Aberdeen was complaining nonstop.

She whined, "Why do we have to go to sleep like old people. It's only one in the morning."

"You are more than welcome to go back out to the bars. I'm not stopping you," I replied.

I couldn't have given two-shits about what she wanted to do.

Once we got in the hotel room, Aberdeen and I both got ready for bed. After I had brushed my teeth, Aberdeen came over and laid down next to me. Even though we were both drunk, I was just not in the mood to hook up with her. She had disrespected my friends and complained the entire night. There wasn't any appreciation from her whatsoever for the drinks or the hotel room.

Aberdeen turned to me and said, "I'm really sorry about tonight. I know now why you are upset with me. I think it was just the alcohol talking."

I replied, "I forgive you but do you realize that what you said was insulting and rude?"

"Yes, and I'm very sorry."

All of a sudden, probably because she was drunk and felt bad, Aberdeen reached under the covers and began to excite the one thing that had been limp all night. She knew that this would probably put a smile on my face and I tried to resist the temptation.

Ok fine let it rip. Wow my self-control sucks.

She began to give me an old-fashioned hand job. I wasn't opposed to this in any way, but her hand felt a bit like sandpaper. As much as it hurt, I felt that I could suffer through the pain for the greatness that hopefully lied ahead. She must have tugged on that skin rope for about fifteen minutes. The absence of a lubricated liquid made it difficult to proceed forward into the grand finale.

Aberdeen said, "My arm hurts. Can we stop?"

I am guessing she is not ambidextrous?

I had to pitch a red flannel tent for about an hour until my woody decided to bow out.

Well that was horrible.

The next morning, we woke up and got breakfast at the hotel. It was still strange that I was never able to get a 'Thank You' for anything. Not only was she non-appreciative, it also seemed that she really didn't know the value of a hard-earned dollar.

After that weekend, I was pretty fed up with her. How could someone so pretty be so shitty? Was her beauty worth all the anguish and frustration?

A few days later, I was talking to Aberdeen on the phone and I was on my way to have some drinks with some of my coworkers.

She asked, "What are doing this weekend?"

I replied, "I'm free Friday but Saturday I have a family dinner."

"Oh ok, well I have plans on Friday. Do you want to hang out on Sunday?"

"Sure that sounds good."

I figured I would give her one more shot before ending the dubious saga.

Aberdeen had plans to go downtown Friday. The details were unknown to me but she sent me a picture of her in a skintight red dress. She looked damn good.

I texted her, "Must be a special occasion. You look gorgeous!"

She texted back, "Thank you. Yeah, kind of LOL."

Whatever the hell that meant. I told her to call me if she needed a ride home from the bar that night.

She texted back, "Yeah I might need one but I must warn you. I will be drunk, and I may jump your bones."

I replied, "Ha-ha. Alrighty then."

That night I didn't receive a single text or a phone call. I was hoping nothing bad happened to her.

The next day, my phone didn't ring once. Maybe she had lost her phone or it was dead for some reason. I didn't want to call and bother her. I figured that she would call me sooner or later. Then on the informative newsfeed of 'Facebook,' the truth was revealed.

'Aberdeen Roberts is in a relationship with Zack Smith.'

The status update also included a picture of the two of them with a heart symbol as the caption. She was wearing the same red dress that I had seen earlier. I guess that Friday was the night they consummated their love for each other.

Wow, didn't see that coming. I cut off communication with Aberdeen even though it seemed she had already done that with me. Maybe it was a blessing in disguise.

I didn't deserve that shit. I was angry but the sadness was outweighing it. It was time to forget everything we had. As long as I could detach myself from her before it became too painful, I would move on with my life much easier.

A few days later, Aberdeen posted pictures of her partying on Zach's fifty-foot yacht on the lake. The picture's caption was, "Hanging out with the BF on his boat! Can't believe it's been six months with this hunk. Love you!"

What the fuck?

I REALLY didn't see that coming.

Apparently, they had been dating the whole time I was seeing her. I had no clue. I guess my job was done. Aberdeen already had a man who apparently had endless amounts of money and a high tolerance for her bullshit. I didn't have either of those.

I was just a side dish.

I began to feel that I just wasn't good enough. My depression kept growing but I felt that there had to be a reason why I was getting run the fuck over by these women. I didn't want to give up on love. I wanted to eventually find the woman who I was meant to be with it. I had no idea it would be this hard. The future looked bleak but I kept living my life as best I could without hanging on to the painful memories of my past.

Chapter 12-Chandler 'The Personal Trainer Sex Fiend'

I decided to take a different approach this time and enroll in an online dating website.

I know what you are thinking. I was just desperate. You are correct.

I figured I would give it a try and take a chance on love with a complete stranger over the Internet. It was always hard to know exactly what to write on your dating profile. I didn't want to be too cocky but also didn't want to come off as an idiot.

Some girls just laid it all out there.

One profile read, "I would just like to get laid before I die."

I didn't know nursing homes had Internet access. I quickly changed my settings on the age range.

Once my profile was set up for about a day, I received a hit. This was strange because typically the guys go after the girls, not vice versa. Something told me that the aggressive nature of this woman was a red flag but what did I have to lose?

My life...possibly.

Her name was Chandler. She was a light-skinned brunette who was a personal trainer. She was my age, which was a plus. She also had some of the same interests as me according to her profile.

We began to chat over the dating website and eventually exchanged numbers. We then started texting each other for a few days and finally agreed to meet for dinner. I picked out a Japanese place that was halfway between her house and mine. I arrived at the restaurant about ten minutes early and walked inside to grab a table.

I let Chandler know that I had arrived via text message, but there was no response. I waited not twenty, not thirty, but forty-five minutes before she arrived.

During my time spent at the table alone, the waitress kept coming by asking me if I needed anything. At one point she even asked, "Is your date coming?"

I replied, "I think so?"

People who can't be on time piss me off.

Chandler finally showed up and apologized several times.

She said, "I feel awful for being so late. I'm terribly sorry."

I replied, "It's ok, I got to know our waitress pretty well, and I got caught up on my reading."

She gave me this blank face.

I chuckled, "I'm kidding. Let's eat!"

I was starving, and I made sure we ordered our food quickly. We then started to get to know each other at the table.

I asked, "So how do you like your profession?"

"Well I have about twenty-five clients, so it keeps me busy. I enjoy it very much," Chandler replied.

Chandler was pretty pleasant to be around. She did however, seem a little wound up. Her hands were shaking when she was taking a sip of her drink, and her eyes were wondering in every direction.

Hopefully she's not an alcoholic.

She was talking erratically. She would say in one breath, "Do you like dogs? I have two dogs. I don't like cats. Cats are mean. What are you getting to eat?"

I couldn't keep up with conversation.

Our food arrived, and Chandler began to scarf down her main dish like she was a garbage disposal. We had ordered a plate for two, and I had to extract my portion with haste in order to have some for myself. There was no time wasted whatsoever in devouring her plate of shrimp fried rice.

I was never opposed to dating a girl with an appetite, but at least take the time to enjoy the food. Don't just cram it down your throat in ten seconds like Cookie Monster.

After we finished our meal, Chandler looked over at me and said, "Let's get the check and go back to my place."

Jesus Christ woman!

She arrived forty-five minutes late, ate her food in a matter of seconds, and now she wanted to tango on a full stomach? The mental image of Chandler vomiting fried rice on me during sex immediately popped into my head.

I know most guys would probably saddle up quick to lay the pipe down with this woman, but I respectfully declined her invitation.

I had a bad feeling about her.

I feared that maybe she was a first class nympho, which meant that she probably had one, if not many, sexually transmitted diseases.

I walked her back to her car and before she got in she said, "Can I see you tomorrow?"

Oh shit. Looks like we have a clingy schizoid on deck.

I calmly told her, "I'm busy until the weekend. Maybe we can go out on Friday?"

"I don't know if I can wait until then, but I'll try."

My God.

We both headed home and that was it for night number one.

For the rest of the week, I received so many text messages from Chandler, I thought for sure my cell phone would explode. She blew up my phone up every five minutes, and it was beginning to get annoying as hell. I was so close to calling the whole thing off, but I figured like I always do…I would give her one last chance.

Reluctant as ever, I suggested that we could go see a movie together and then get drinks afterwards. I drove out to her place to pick her up. Chandler got in the car and instantaneously began to 'jack her jaw' like she did before.

She was going on and on about multiple subjects which I had absolutely no interest in. Things like shopping, clothes, and other dumb shit. I couldn't tell you exactly how many topics she covered, because I wasn't really paying attention. Then all of a sudden, the dreaded words came out of her mouth.

"Juddy, I need to be honest with you," she said.

Jesus, I'm sick of hearing that shit.

Chandler revealed, "I just want to be upfront with you. I have slept with a lot of guys."

I replied, "Um, ok. May I ask how many?"

"About seventy I think. I just want to be completely open with you."

HOLY FUCK BALLS!

I knew I had to get the hell out of this fast. Lord only knows what hideous and disgusting things lurk inside her subterranean zone. I was not about to strap on a hardhat and go dumpster diving.

For the rest of the night, I was completely emotionless. I wanted to make sure she knew I had absolutely zero interest in her.

Once we got to the movie theatre, I quickly looked up on my phone how long the film was going to be.

Two hours and thirty minutes? Son-of-a-bitch.

At least we were in an environment where there was no talking allowed. Chandler kept trying to lean against me and hold my hand but I shut her down every time.

Once the movie was over she asked, "How about those drinks?"

I replied, "I'm sorry. I got a call from work during the movie. I have to go in at 5am tomorrow. I need to head home early and get some sleep."

I could tell quickly that she was pissed. Her eyebrows suddenly became diagonal. Maybe I was the first guy to hold up the stop sign to the sex fiend freight train. The whole way home, she kept asking me to stay the night at her place. I started to drive faster to get things over with. I pulled up to her apartment and before she got out she said, "I don't know why you just don't come up for one drink."

Everybody knows it's never just one drink.

I replied, "I'm sorry. I promise we will have drinks next time."

Once I dropped her off, I felt like a free man, and I was ready to move on with my life. I thought the nightmare was over, but it wasn't.

The next few days, things became quite hostile between Chandler and I. The battle zone was none other than the world of text messages, where true feelings can be expressed without being face-to-face.

Since Chandler and I were both connected on the same dating website, she had seen that I had been active on the site after our second date possibly looking for other women. That same day, I received one of the weirdest text messages ever…

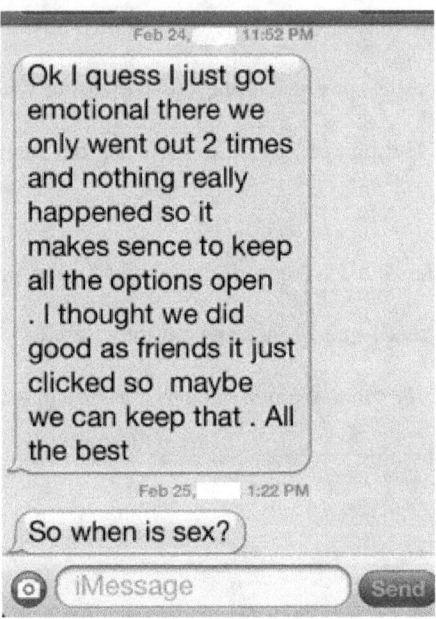

How does that make any sense? In the first text, she wished me the best. Like we were finished. Then twenty-four hours later, she is asking me 'When is sex?'

Why would I want to have sex with someone who has slept with more people than I probably will in my entire lifetime?

Plus, statistically speaking, she was guaranteed to have one or multiple STD's. Sex was the last thing on my mind with Chandler so I didn't respond. Then a day later, she fired back at me again.

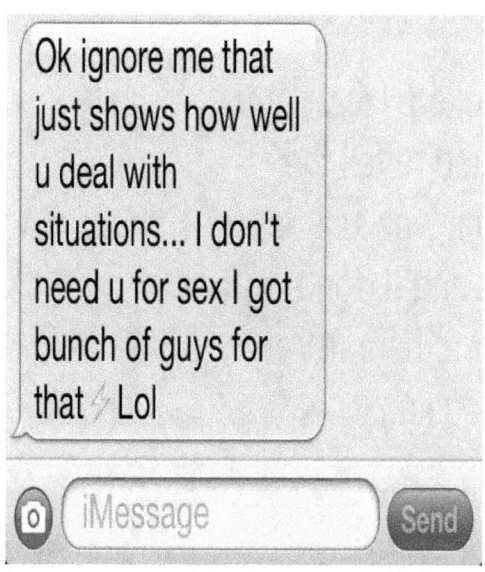

I would agree that this concubine doesn't need me for sex so why was she bothering me? Also what was the deal with the fucking lightning bolt? Why the hell was she laughing?

I was sharing these texts over 'Facebook,' and everyone was getting a kick out of them, so I decided to fish for one more insane text to end the saga of slutiness.

I finally wrote Chandler back and asked, "I thought we really had good chemistry and everything went really well. Didn't you?"

She responded…

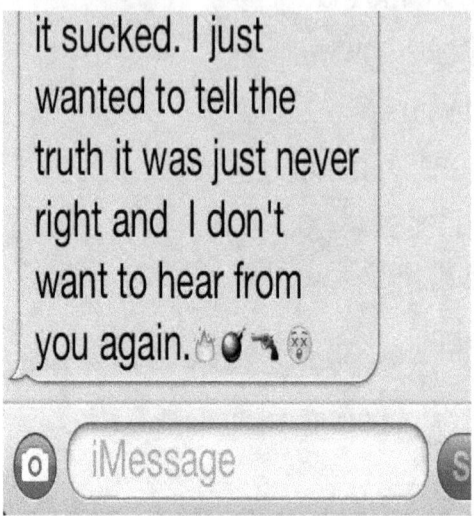

That was the last communication I ever received from her. I was praying that Chandler found the dark hole that she crawled out of and locked herself inside forever.

Crazy bitch.

Chapter 13-Fawn 'The Wasted Witch'

One of my good friends Melissa sent me a message on 'Facebook' one day. She had known about my continued trouble with women and just wanted to help. She had a close friend that she thought would be a perfect match.

She said, "Check her out! She is really cute and a goofball! I think you two would totally hit it off!"

I've heard that tagline about a million times before but it's usually just a disaster waiting to happen.

Her name was Fawn

In my preliminary 'Facebook' stalking, I examined her profile thoroughly. She had long blonde hair, light skin, green eyes, and long legs. She towered over her friends in most of her pictures. I was praying she wasn't taller than me.

Giant women are intimidating but doable.

She was a Special Ed schoolteacher, and about two years younger than me. I sent her a friend request to break the social media ice. We began to 'Facebook' chat back and forth and eventually exchanged numbers.

We decided to meet up for dinner at a local Mexican restaurant. It was a family owned place that was pretty small and not too far of a drive.

When I arrived, I could smell the fresh tortillas and refried beans in the air. It was a place of carbs, heartburn, and possibly… romance.

I sat down at a booth near the back of the restaurant and patiently waited. Fawn wasn't far behind me. She arrived about ten minutes later.

She had on a button down white linen shirt, jean shorts, and sandals. She had her hair down and didn't have too much makeup on. She was naturally beautiful, and I was impressed.

I stood up and introduced myself. There was an awkward moment where I didn't know whether to shake her hand or give her a friendly hug.

"Hello, Fawn. I'm, Juddy," I nervously said.

I leaned in to go for the hug and almost tripped over her long legs. I barreled into her almost knocking her over.

"I'm so sorry," I said.

She chuckled, "No problem."

Off to a great start.

Fawn said, "I love these little places. They always have the best food."

I replied, "Oh yes. I think we're in good hands."

Fawn was pretty damn funny. She was quick to the draw with humorous comebacks and jokes.

I told her, "Thanks for joining me tonight. I was anxious to meet you in person."

"I don't ever pass up a free dinner with complementary margaritas. Ha-ha. Just kidding," she replied.

She had an outgoing personality like me. I began to feel more comfortable at the small table filled with chips and queso.

Having endured many horrible relationships over the years, I found myself in a different frame of mind that night. As I was gazing at Fawn, I wasn't thinking about if she was girlfriend material, our possible future together, or even what she looked like naked.

I had only one question on my mind. How would she fuck me over? It's inevitable and always has been for me.

"This is my second celebration today!" Fawn proudly said.

"What was your first?" I asked.

"I sold my condo today and I went to have drinks afterwards."

"You had drinks with your realtor?"

"No silly. Drinks by myself."

Oh shit.

Our frozen margaritas showed up quickly to the table. Fawn grabbed hers, and began to suck it down like it was a spring break contest. I thought that the brain-freeze effect would kick in, and temporarily disengage her tequila slushy guzzling. Apparently she had developed immunity to it, and finished half of the Mexican goblet in a matter of seconds.

She said, "That margarita wasn't very strong. How is yours?"

I hadn't even had time to indulge in mine so I took a sip.

I replied, "It's quite strong to me."

"Oh come on, Grandpa. Suck it up!"

She then ordered a shot of tequila to add to her already booze filled drink. I had just met this girl, so I wasn't use to her overall behavior, but something told me that she was about to fly off the handle.

In my experience if it starts with tequila, it will end with bloodshed.

Fawn poured the shot into her drink and gave it a finger swirl, even though she could have politely used the straw. After she finished the large bowl of tequila and frozen limejuice, she ordered another one.

"Yes can I get another large margarita with an extra shot of tequila? Do you want another one, Juddy? Sorry, I'm just really thirsty," she said.

"I'm ok. I'm still working on my first one," I mumbled.

"You drink like a turtle."

I couldn't quite grasp her logic at first. I know turtles are slow movers, but do they also consume liquid at a leisurely pace?

"I guess your implying that I drink slowly?" I asked.

"Yes I am," she chuckled.

Fawn was beginning to get rather sloppy. Her eyes were shot to bloody hell, and she had a hard time matching her mouth to the straw. It was if the straw itself had a mind of its own, and it just didn't want to suffer anymore.

Once our fajitas for two arrived, we both started to dig in.

Due to Fawn's level of intoxication, she was unable to construct a complete fajita burrito without making a complete mess. After many failed attempts, she decided to use the provided utensils to consume the meal. Her fork was missing her mouth with every other bite. There were food particles scattered all over the table. It looked like a bomb had exploded that was packed with beans, rice, and meat. Fawn even had small pieces of rice stuck in her hair. It was like watching a small child eat solid food for the very first time.

She slowly gathered all of the food debris like a starving homeless woman and consumed every last bite. She then set her sights back on her second margarita, which was almost empty.

Fawn asked, "Do you have time for one more drink?"

I said, "Yeah sure, but I would hold off on another extra shot of tequila. You're beating me in this drinking game we have going on, and I need to catch up."

That was a nice way of me saying slowdown dingbat.

"You're funny. I'm just going to have one more margarita and one more shot."

"That is the exact opposite of what I just said."

"Ha-ha. You're silly."

God, help me.

At this point it started to get awkward. She began to deep throat her third large margarita. Her laughter was beginning to morph into something evil. It sounded like the cackling of the witch in the 'Wizard of Oz.' She also began to slur her words horrendously.

She asked, "Soooooo what are yooou doing t'night?"

I confusingly replied, "Well I'm here with you so that's about it."

"You'reeeeee funnyyyyy. HA-HA-HA-HA!"

Her laughter became so loud and horrifying, a small child about two tables down began to cry. Fawn's eyes began to roll into the back of her head. She was barely able to sit up straight and people began to stare. Her head was tipping in every direction. It almost looked like I was performing an exorcism. I was quite embarrassed, and just wanted to leave.

However, there was no way I was letting her drive anywhere.

I calmly said, "Fawn I have to use the restroom real quick. I already paid the bill. I think it's best if I drove you home tonight."

She replied, "I can driiive just fiiiine."

"I would feel much better if I gave you a ride home."

"Ugh…fiiiine whateverrrrr."

As I walked away, Fawn was falling over the table. It looked like she was on a ship that was being pummeled by numerous waves. She was clinging onto the table like it was a personal flotation device.

I went into the restroom and contemplated how the hell I was going to drag her 'punch-drunk' ass out of there. She was two-breaths away from being unconscious, and I just wanted to get her home safe.

There I am. Mr. Nice Guy to the fucking rescue once again.

I came back to the table. Fawn was gone and she had left her purse on her seat.

Where the hell did she go? Maybe she just went to the bathroom? Why would she leave her purse?

I asked the waitress, "Excuse me, did you see where my date went?"

The waitress said, "Sir, she went out the front door about five minutes ago.

Oh shit. This is bad.

I frantically ran outside with Fawn's purse in my hand. All of a sudden a black car emerged from the parking lot. It was Fawn. She was driving past the front door of the restaurant. I ran out into the street to try to stop her. As she flew right by me in her Honda Civic, she blew me a kiss.

What the fuck?

She violently swerved out of parking lot without even applying the brakes. Fawn's car then smashed right into the passenger side of an oncoming vehicle that was going about thirty miles per hour. The sound of the metal clashing was extremely loud and engine smoke began to fill the air from Fawn's vehicle.

The employees from the restaurant came outside to see what happened. Meanwhile, I was staring in shock holding Fawn's purse in my hands. I wanted so badly to drop the purse and bail, but I knew I had to do the right thing.

I immediately ran over to the crime scene to see if everyone was ok. Fawn's airbag had deployed, and her front bumper was demolished. I opened the car door to get her out. Fawn's face was covered in airbag powder. I wiped away most of it, and underneath the white dust, she was laughing.

What the fuck is wrong with this woman?

"Fawn, you have been in a car accident. Are you ok?" I asked.

"Yes, dummy. I'm totally cool," she chuckled.

I went over to the other vehicle. There was a forty-year-old man in the driver seat of a Toyota Camry. His passenger side door was completely caved in.

I asked him. "Are you ok, sir?"

He replied in shock, "Yeah…I'm fine. Thank you."

"I'll call 911."

I went back over to Fawn.

I explained, "Fawn, any minute the cops are going to show up. There is no easy way to say this. You're going to be arrested. You must refuse every test the cops attempt to give you. You will then go to jail and be released in the morning."

She then unbuttoned her shirt and exposed her bra, which had a good built in cleavage support system.

Fawn replied, "What if I just show the cops my tits?"

I replied, "Those are very lovely, but they're not going to help you one bit. I need you to find your insurance papers."

She slowly wobbled over to the passenger side of her car like a zombie. Her face was still covered in airbag dust. She reached in the glove box, and pulled out a fat stack of coffee stained bound paper. She then handed it over to me.

I said, "Fawn, this is the owner's manual for your car."

She chuckled, "Whoopsies!"

Jesus Christ.

The cops arrived. They began to question Fawn, the other driver, and myself. I told them exactly what I saw without revealing that I was the asshole that fed her three gigantic margaritas, which prompted the car crash. The cops also spoke to a few of the employees that confirmed the story of the crazed female on a 'highway to hell.'

Against my recommendation. Fawn agreed to perform the field sobriety tests.

This was going to be a shit show.

The first test the cops were going to administer was the one legged countdown. Fawn was instructed to stand on one leg and count from ten, down to one.

She hopped up on one leg and began the test. Her body was swaying back and forth. Her raised leg was flying all over the place, and she was fighting for her life to stay balanced. It was like watching a drunken acrobat.

She began to count off but was going the wrong direction.

"10-11-12-13-14-15," she sounded off.

Swing and a miss.

The next one up was the finger to nose test. She was instructed to stand up straight, and count from one to ten. As she counted each number, she had to switch arms and touch the tip of her nose. She failed to touch her nose once. Instead, her finger would either land on her chin or her forehead. Also, rather than stopping at ten, she kept going all the way up to twenty until the cop stopped her.

Another crash and burn.

The final test was the pen test. She was instructed to follow the pen from left to right with her eyes while keeping her head still. She followed the pen with her head the entire time. Never once did she use her eyes to successfully complete the test. She looked like an android that was malfunctioning.

Fawn was then put in handcuffs and arrested. Before they hauled her away, I went over to the cops to give them Fawn's purse which had all of her belongings in it. As I was handing over the bag there was a side pouch that had come open. A few things tumbled out of it during the transfer of goods. Among the objects that fell to the ground were two empty mini bottles of white wine, which I'm guessing Fawn drank before dinner.

The hits just kept coming.

Both of the cars were towed away, Fawn headed to the slammer, and I went home. The whole way home, I felt a bit responsible for letting Fawn get way too drunk. I had no clue how many drinks she had consumed before she met up with me. At the same time, she was a grown woman, but something told me she was a frequent heavy drinker.

I don't know…call it a hunch.

When I got home, I fell asleep with a sense of guilt on my mind. There was really nothing I could do now, except wait for a phone call.

The next day at 6am, I was awoken by one of the strangest phone calls of my life.

It was an unknown number, so at first I thought it was Fawn calling from jail. I answered the phone.

"Hello?" I said.

"Yes, Juddy. This is Vikki Mullins, Fawn's mother. I know this is quite awkward, but Fawn said that she was going to be staying the night with you last night. I just wanted to make sure she made it to work on time this morning."

Oh man. She has no idea. Well I'm about to turn her shit upside down.

I replied, "Fawn won't be able to make it to work today Mrs. Thompson. She's safe, but she's in jail. She was involved in car accident but everyone was ok. Unfortunately, Fawn was arrested for driving while intoxicated. I'm so sorry."

She chuckled, "Well that doesn't surprise me. It was bound to happen sooner or later."

What the hell is wrong with these people?

I gave her all the details and told her to call me if she needed any help getting her daughter released.

I never heard from Fawn again.

After the worst date of my life was over, the days began to become dark. This was the final lashing of my torturous love life. I was slipping fast into a world I had tried to avoid my entire life. It was filled with hatred, anger, and sadness. Everything around me began to collapse, and I couldn't keep myself together anymore. I was struggling to grasp onto something that would keep me from going insane. Nothing in my life was making sense anymore, and I was struggling to cope with the loneliness.

Chapter 14-Love Is Dangerous

Days went by as I slowly began to become a recluse. I was hiding from the outside world and afraid of what the future held for me. The emotional bullets that had penetrated my skin over the years had buried themselves deep within my heart.

I kept asking myself did I pull the trigger?

The future looked like a long field covered in fog. I couldn't see what lied ahead, but I knew I would face it alone. My parents taught me everything there was to know about being a gentleman, yet I was never taught how to deal with a breakup. I was struggling with depression, and I had no idea how to stop it from growing. I was beginning to sink into a dark world, and I didn't think I would make it much longer.

Day in and day out, the horrible memories of my past were running circles in my head. There were so many questions and not enough answers. I felt that I really couldn't approach anyone about it. I didn't want to bother my family or friends with these burdens. They were mine and mine alone. Hope was slowly vanishing into thin air. I felt like I was hanging by a thread, and sooner or later, I would snap and be forever consumed by sadness.

My life of solitude went from weeks to months. My physical health also began to decline. I started drinking heavily, and my sleep was being severely affected. I didn't have the strength to exercise, so I started to put on a lot of weight. My beard and mustache were growing out because I didn't feel like shaving anymore. It became scraggly and coarse. I just flat out stopped taking care of myself, and I closely resembled Tom Hanks from 'Cast Away.' Only I was about forty pounds heavier. With my declining health, the depression became worse, and I didn't know where to turn.

The only answer I could find was…more alcohol.

One night, I decided to take a drive to a local dive bar. It was a small Irish pub that I began to frequent to drown my feelings on a regular basis. It was dump, and that's why I loved going there.

On the inside the bar there were old wooden stools scattered about, a few televisions from the early 80's, and pool table covered in dust.

As I walked to find a table, the smell of cigarette smoke, and old cedar wood filled my nostrils. There were a couple of weary men at the bar having a few cold ones. They looked exhausted and beat up from head to toe after a hard day's work.

I should fit right in.

I didn't feel like talking to anyone so I picked out a small booth towards the back of the bar. It was a dimly lit area accompanied with a small lamp that was hanging from the ceiling. I sat down and embraced the dark corner of the old pub.

A waitress came up to me shortly after I sat down. She was wearing a T-shirt with raggedy looking jeans. She was a pretty girl, but she was the fucking enemy.

She asked, "Will there be anybody else joining you tonight?"

I said, "Only one of my good pals, Mr. Jack Daniels."

"Coming right up."

The waitress quickly came back with a small Mason jar of the famous brown cough medicine. The glass looked like it hadn't been washed in awhile, but I didn't care. I stared at the dark poison for a bit without drinking a sip. All I saw inside was destruction and failure. The emotional torture that was inflicted by these women had finally ripped my heart in two.

I lifted the glass off of the old wooden table. I needed to go back to the very beginning of this terrible nightmare. Only there would I find what I was looking for.

Once the whiskey traveled down my throat, I began to unravel the reasons why I was slowly going insane.

Jayden was labeled as the 'untouchable angel.' I was intrigued by her brains and amazed at how white her teeth were.

I believe that Jayden chose me because I was the only one not begging for her attention. I was a good chase for her. She had to work for it. Just like her 4.0 GPA.

I was hoping the relationship would continue through college. She was my very first love, and I felt compelled to save us because I believed we had something very special. I wanted our good memories to continue, but my naive nature was crippling my judgment.

Unfortunately, Jayden had other plans.

I believe the reason she wanted to break up before college was to be free. Free from a boyfriend, free from her parents rules, and free to do anything she wanted.

After her mental breakdown, I decided to get back together with her because I believed if I didn't, she would kill herself. If something bad happened to her, the guilt would shadow me forever and I would never forgive myself. Not to mention the blame her parents and everyone who knew us would've placed upon me.

It was sympathetic love and nothing more.

Jayden came back to me because she was desperate and in denial. She also needed a scapegoat to protect her perfect image so her parents wouldn't think less of her.

I was her whipping boy.

Everything around her was crumbling down and I think she believed that rekindling our relationship would be the first step in becoming normal again.

"Here's to you, Jayden. Thank you for taking my virginity and my dignity."

I ordered another whiskey.

Next up was the long legged crack head. Ravenna was unique in more ways than one. I was hoping for something new and exciting when I met her. After a few weeks, the relationship was on its merry way and we had a lot fun times together.

After meeting Ravenna's father, it seemed the men of her past were all pieces of shit. I felt it was my duty to bring out the very best in Ravenna. To show her parents she could date a good guy who would make her happy. I also felt sympathetic after the revelation of her car accident.

Ravenna kept me around to win over the affection of her parents. After the DWI, her parents had a tainted view of their daughter. If she had a good man in the picture, her parents would gain the confidence they once had in their only daughter. She needed me to be a temporary knight in shining armor. I felt that I was being courageous, but I was just getting used.

Once she was done faking it to please her parents, she got off with her drug-dealing ex-boyfriend.

"Here's to you, Ravenna. Please stop snorting blow and banging drug dealers."

In a deep barbaric voice I said, "Another whiskey waitress! I'm just getting started!"

The waitress gave me a weird look and brought me another drink.

Ah, yes. The snake.

She struck when I least expected it, and she struck hard, while stroking another guy.

Sydnie was the cute blue-eyed girl in my Geography class. I saw an opportunity, and I went for it.

We seemed to get along very well. We liked the same movies, food, and TV shows. We just clicked.

She blindsided me underneath the same fucking roof. Sydnie, I guess felt sorry for the circus freak. He probably hadn't been laid in awhile, and she was kind enough to oblige him twenty feet away from where I was sleeping. I thought we had a healthy relationship with a lot of good memories, but there was nothing to prepare me for what happened inside that beach house. Maybe she was just bored, drunk, and horny. What a blind fool I was.

"Here's to you, Sydnie. Sucks to be a slut."

I needed two drinks for the next one. I was going into the deep abyss now.

Next was the violent one. The nutcase. The evil gremlin.

There were many names for her. She had multiple identities that changed at the drop of a shot glass.

Gretchen was pretty quiet and low key at first. I thought she was just shy and had a good personality inside waiting to be unlocked.

Upon meeting her father, I believed Gretchen may have been raised in an abusive home. This could have caused her to violently lash out at me from time to time while intoxicated. I felt I could help her deal with her issues and morph her into something opposite of what her father was. Maybe the yelling and screaming was how her father communicated to her as a child. As the violent tirades became worse, the family genetics became more visible.

I was afraid of the fact that this might have been my last chance at love. Everyone around me at the time had a significant other. I felt like I deserved to be with someone. My mind was warped by delusions of grandeur, and I had tunnel vision. I couldn't quite grasp how bad the relationship really was until it was too late.

Gretchen wanted someone to blame for her own downfalls. She couldn't face her own insecurities, and there were many of them.

Instead, she made me feel like a piece of shit. She manipulated my reality until I thought I was the sole cause for her tyrannical psychotic behavior. She was afraid that people would find out what kind of monster she really was. Behind closed doors, I was the one that suffered her violent wrath.

"Here's to you Gretchen. You might want to stop drinking…like forever."

I was getting drunker by the minute, but I still had some ground to cover. I kept going.

Next up was the virtual girlfriend.

The one and only blind date turned out to be one hell of a night. As I got to know Carlisle through the weeks passing by, she was probably the closest thing to a perfect match with regards to her personality. Although her Internet based profession put a bad taste in my mouth, I enjoyed my time with her. I thought even though she was fresh out of a relationship things for us were moving in a good direction. I respected her because she was self-employed, and I thought that we would have a future together.

I was just a rebound for Carlisle. Plain and simple. She obviously still had feelings for her ex, and I was just in the wrong place at the wrong time. Once she was with me, she realized how important her ex was to her. She decided to keep me around until I took off.

Another whiskey down the esophagus.

Next up was the two-faced ice-dancing queen.

When first meeting Aberdeen, I could tell that she had her nose up in the air. At first, I thought it was an act to shield her from the various assholes around the globe.

Maybe she was just protecting herself?

I began to date her to see if I could find out truly who she was and if we were meant to be together. Obviously we weren't.

She reminded me a little of Jayden. I wasn't begging for Aberdeen's attention, and I wasn't on my hands and knees. I was simply present.

Aberdeen sensed I was being evasive right off the bat. I believe that she enjoyed the chase. You always want what you can't have, and clearly, Aberdeen was accustomed to always getting what she wanted.

She got rid of me quick and sailed off into the sunset on her boyfriend's yacht.

Put another whiskey on the board for me.

Next up was the nympho.

Chandler was definitely a character. Honestly, I was desperate at the time and figured I would give online dating a try. That was a big mistake.

As for Chandler, well, the question still remains.

"When is sex?"

Last but not least was the jolly ol'drunken witch.

Fawn obviously had a major drinking problem. I was fearful of her safety, and I'm glad that she wasn't seriously injured in the car accident. I wouldn't be surprised if she was still in prison.

From time to time I still hear her evil cackling laugh in my nightmares.

I was high and dry and needed another drink. My speech was beginning to slur like a mumbling fool, and my vision was massively impaired. I was just waiting for the moment where the waitress would cut me off from my whiskey bloodbath.

She came over to me and said, "I'm sorry you have had so much trouble with women."

I blurted out, "How do you know that?"

"You have been talking out loud this whole time."

"Shit."

"This next drink is on me. Just promise you won't drive home."

"But of course."

Before I picked up the next drink, I began to sink into a black hole. I was going down to the very depths of what really needed to be discovered. It was a deserted place, and had not been explored in many years. I had closed off the gates to my heart in order to protect my feelings and my secrets.

I needed to dig deep in order to find everything I did wrong. I needed to know why I failed as a boyfriend.

What madness did I drive these women to? Was this all my fault?

As I started to walk down the dark road on my self-destructive journey, the first stop I came across was the lack of honesty.

I wasn't honest with any of these women or myself. I neglected to inform them of how I really felt. I was ashamed, depressed, and I felt like a prisoner. There were many things they did that would upset me or anger me. I figured, why bring it up and start a fight?

Instead of making my voice heard, I buried my feelings inside and threw away any real emotion I ever had. I put on a show for everyone. I didn't want anyone to know how rotten I felt on the inside.

I was pretending to be happy just to make things run smoothly. I should have been upfront about certain aspects of the relationship that I was uncomfortable with. Maybe if I had voiced my concerns about the troubled relationship known, it would've saved me from a few heartaches. I thought I was happy, but I was lying the whole time.

Next up would be communication, which goes hand in hand with honesty. I didn't communicate my feelings properly to these women nor to myself. They needed to know I wasn't happy. They also needed to know exactly what I was uncomfortable with. This also kept me from getting to know these women for who they really were. By effectively communicating, I could've easily determined that these women were not meant for me, nor I for them. I tried to listen to their needs and wants, but never presented my feelings as a boyfriend. My failure to communicate undoubtedly sent many mixed signals to all of these women.

The road was becoming darker and colder.

The third downfall of mine would be trust. How could I trust the next girl when every single one before had fucked me over?

I don't think I ever truly trusted any of them.

At times, I believed I called too much or text messaged too much. I was also too clingy, but that was who I had become after many unfaithful episodes. Most of the time, all I wanted to know was that they made it home safe.

If I didn't trust them I shouldn't have been with them. When I decided to take the chance of putting trust in these women it was soon decimated into a thousand pieces. I would then try to put myself back together hoping that I would be strong enough to survive the next emotional catastrophe.

I had trouble trusting these women because 'being cheated on' became commonplace for me. It almost became normal. I figured that this kind of shit happens to everyone out there, and it's just a part of the battle.

One big mistake was trusting Gretchen after she cheated on me the first time. I would always wonder where she was after that. In my mind, every time she wasn't with me, the fear of cheating flooded my brain. I should've dumped her right then and there.

I should only trust those who deserve my trust, and obviously none of these women did.

I have trust issues and most likely I always will.

The next stop along this path of failures was my infatuation with beauty. I had a desire to date the best looking girl I could find. I would often be drawn to the girl by her beauty on the outside, without ever finding out exactly who she was on the inside.

Lust is one of the seven deadly sins, and I was unknowingly becoming consumed by it. My physical attraction heavily outweighed the emotional attraction, which caused me to make poor decisions.

Some of the best looking girls where inherently the worst.

The fifth downfall was the premature exposure of my undying love. I wore my heart out on my sleeve, but never guarded it. I didn't get to know these women before I inserted myself deep within their love life. I just wanted to find love, but I was rushing it. I just needed to let it happen. I set myself up easily for heartbreak. I fell too hard and too damn fast.

Coming up at the end of my dark path was a bridge I almost didn't want to cross but I knew I had to. I tipped back one final swig and began to expose my final weakness.

I was…a fucking coward. I never stood up for myself. To them I was a safety valve, a last resort, and a no risk investment. I degraded myself as a man at the same time. There were no repercussions whatsoever for the terrible things they did. I was always there waiting and willing to be the best boyfriend I could be even at the expense of my dignity. I lacked confidence in myself, and these women were fully aware of it.

I also let these women walk all over me. It was like getting punched in the nuts over and over again. No matter what they did to me, I never turned my back on them during the relationship.

To put it simply, I was…a pussy.

After the dismembering of my inner self, all the mistakes I had made during the long road of relationships had finally been brought to the surface.

I was 'dipshit drunk' and ready to go home.

As I lifted my head up off the wooden table, I happened to notice something strange. There was someone sitting across from me but I couldn't see who it was.

"Hello, Juddy."

"Who the hell are you?"

"I am the one responsible for all your pain, all your anger, and all of your failures. My name…is Mr. Nice Guy."

He then leaned into the light revealing his face. I almost didn't recognize him.

It was the older version of me…in the flesh; way before this nightmare even began.

"Do you know how badly I want to kill you?" I uttered with anger in my eyes.

He replied, "Yes, but if you kill me, you will destroy the gentlemen you have been raised to be.

"I don't give a fuck anymore. You have been the sole cause for every terrible thing that has ever happened to me. You are a coward and a liar. I fucking hate you!"

"Without me you will become evil. Cruelty will run through your veins. You will embrace apathy and will forever be alone."

"So be it."

"You must learn from what I did wrong. You must become a better man. A wiser man. A stronger man"

"I never want to be like you. It is YOU that did this shit to me. And now it's time for you to feel my pain!"

A large butcher knife appeared my right hand. I lunged forward and pierced the knife as hard as I could into his chest. I twisted it until the handle broke off. Blood spilled onto the table like a crashing wave.

With his dying breath he said, "Goodbye, my friend. Don't lose yourself."

He then disappeared. Mr. Nice Guy was gone.

It felt like a part of me was erased forever. I was confused, but I felt a sense of relief.

What if he was right and I was wrong?

I was completely hammered and I could barely sit up straight. I attempted to call for a ride home from one of buddies but I had forgotten the four-digit password to unlock my damn phone.

Son-of-a-bitch.

Even if I did manage to unlock the phone my vision was extremely impaired. I wouldn't be able to read anything on the small screen anyways.

The waitress came over to close me out.

She said, "You better not be driving anywhere."

I chuckled, "Don't you worry. Where I'm going, I don't need roads."

"What the hell are you talking about?"

"Never mind."

I slowly stumbled out the front door. I knew for sure there was no way I was driving anywhere. My apartment was only a few miles away, and I started to make my shitfaced journey back home.

There weren't any sidewalks so I was just walking on the curb the whole time. During my march of madness, I accidentally stumbled onto the road a few times. There were multiple cars that honked their horns, and yelled things like, "Get off the street you drunk asshole," and "Look at that fucking idiot!"

I had two intersections left before I reached the front of my apartment complex. All of a sudden, I saw a police car coming right for me with its lights on.

Shit what the hell do I do now? They may take me in for Public Intoxication. Maybe I can just explain what's going on, and they will give me a ride to my house.

Fuck that. I started to run.

Have you ever had a dream where you were running as fast as you could but not moving an inch? That is the best way I could have described my Jack Daniels speed shuffle that night.

I was going to run until my heart exploded or until I was caught.

I could hear the officers on their vehicle intercom: "Stop running and get down on the ground!"

I looked back at the car which was about 100 yards away and yelled, "You'll never catch me alive!"

As soon I finished my heroic sentence, I turned around and began to roll down the ditch that was right behind my apartment building. I was tumbling down it like a sack of potatoes. My arms and legs were flinging in every direction like noodles. I looked like Woody from 'Toy Story.'

I finally hit the bottom of the ditch. It had rained earlier that day, so I was covered in mud from head to toe.

I guess this is what they call rock bottom.

I slowly picked myself up from the crevasse of mud. The officers were on foot and coming right for me. As they came to the top of the ditch, they pointed their flashlights right on me. Since my face was covered in mud, and it was late at night, there was a small case of mistaken identity.

"We have one African American male on foot height is about 5'11" possible Public Intoxication," the officer said.

The officers told me to put my hands in the air and slowly walked up to them. I barely made the impossible hike up what felt like a fucking mountain.

Once I got to the top, they put handcuffs on me and began to question me.

They asked, "What the hell are you doing out here son?"

I replied, "I got too drunk at the bar and I didn't want to drive home, so I decided to walk."

"We had reports of a suspicious individual yelling and screaming at cars at the intersections along this road."

"Officer it was probably me. I'm pretty pissed at this one asshole. His name is Mr. Nice Guy. He ruined my life."

They both began to laugh. The officers grabbed my wallet and began to search through it. They found my Police Federal Credit Union ID card.

One of the officers asked, "Are you a police officer?"

I chuckled, "I once was but not anymore."

"What do you do now?"

"I'm just a drunk."

They both started to laugh again.

They said, "We are going to give you a break tonight but don't let this happen again."

"Yes sir. I'm sorry for the trouble," I replied.

The officers took the handcuffs off.

They put me in the back seat of their car and drove me to my apartment building. I thanked them for letting me go and barged into my apartment still covered in mud.

As soon as I walked in, I began to cry uncontrollably. I had never traveled this far into my dark emotional dungeon, and I was starting to become a prisoner in my own depression.

My muddy footprints were tracked all the way to my final resting place, which was a cozy spot on the bathroom floor next to the toilet. With all the wet mud on me, it probably looked like I had shit all over myself and in a sense…I kind of did.

The next morning, I woke up with crusted dirt on my eyelids. My head was pounding and I felt like complete shit. I had crash-landed into my own pit of sorrow. I was deep within the emotional jungle that was filled with all different types of animals and creatures that had tortured me over the years.

All of these women had a hand in my demise, but the exposing of my own failures had brought me to a very dark place.

In that dark place, the nice guy inside me was destroyed. I was consumed with depression, and I couldn't hold myself together as a man anymore. I was trying to stop the pain from destroying my future.

This very well could be the end for me…

Revenge Is Near

I had to make a choice. This decision would affect the rest of my life as I knew it. I could die a lonely man or become stronger than I ever imagined. I wanted to repair the damage that was done and build a new future for myself.

I began to transform the horrible memories I held onto over the years into something that would make people smile. Something that would change the way they looked at relationships…forever.

All of my life I have always dreamed about doing standup comedy. Since the day I was born, I have thoroughly enjoyed making people laugh. If I could create humor out of my dreadful experiences, I could quite possibly help people overcome the pain of a broken heart. Almost everyone on this earth has been involved in a bad relationship, and I wanted to use my stories of misfortune to help them.

I always felt that one of my very best talents was self-degradation in the form of comedic storytelling. By using the painful memories I could create a world of humor for people to experience.

I decided to organize my first standup comedy show.

It definitely took some work to put on. I did everything from reserving the venue, setting up ticket sales online, promoting the show, and writing the show.

I started to write for months trying to come up with the best material I could dig up. I was insanely nervous that the turnout would be disappointing or the jokes would be awful. I worked day and night on material, making sure that the show had a good chance at being successful.

For the longest time, I was having trouble finding a name for the show. Finally, one day it came to me.

My first comedy show 'Revenge' was in full production. There was a huge portion of ex-girlfriend material, so I figured the title was perfect. I mailed out over 500 flyers to all my friends and family in order to sell tickets. The show was six months away, and I had a lot of writing and rehearsing to do.

My reputation was on the line. I was willing to take that risk, and I wasn't going to let anyone stop me. All I knew was that for the first time in my life, I felt that this and always has been my destiny.

As I was rehearsing nonstop and overdosing on coffee, the months flew by. The show was right around the corner and each day I became more anxious. I didn't know how many tickets had been sold because I promised myself I wouldn't look at the number until the day of. I was worried that I would log in online and only see about twenty tickets sold for the event. That would have sucked. The venue I rented was not cheap. The total rental cost was $3,500. I had to pay for that with ticket sales or out of my own pocket if need be.

On the day of the show, for the first time, I saw how many tickets had been sold in order to know how my chairs I needed to set up for the event. I couldn't believe my eyes. The total number of tickets sold was 236.

I was in complete shock. I thought that I would maybe sell 100 at most. This revelation not only made me excited but extremely nervous.

How in God's name am I going to entertain that many people tonight?

I had to summon an old friend of mine for help that night. While I was rehearsing before the show, I threw back three shots of

Jack Daniels as quick as I could. It was about half an hour until show time, and I was frantically pacing backstage.

One of my good friends offered to introduce me that night. He got up on stage, and grabbed the microphone. He told everyone to take their seats, and it became deathly quiet inside the auditorium. The hair on the back of my neck stood up and my shaking hands were covered in sweat.

My friend announced, "Ladies and Gentlemen. Please help me welcome, Juddy Ferguson."

I walked out onto the stage, and to my surprise everyone in the audience got up out of their seats and gave me a standing ovation. It was one the best moments of my life, and I was truly blessed to have the support from friends and family that evening. As soon as I grabbed the microphone, the crowd quickly became silent. I then began to deliver my very first stand-up comedy show…

The material began to flow very well mostly due to the whiskey. I felt so alive on stage. I was doing something that made me happy, and I enjoyed every single minute of it. My subject matter included a day at the zoo, awkward moments, hangovers, and crazy ex-girlfriends.

Of course I left the best for last.

At the tail end of the show, I had about fifteen minutes worth of ex-girlfriend material. Gretchen got it the worst by far, mainly because she did the most psychological damage.

My favorite moment from the show was the encore. Once the main act of the show was over, I thanked everyone for coming and walked off stage. The crowd was cheering and my adrenaline was racing. I came back on stage for one final tale. It was a story that happened long ago and it involved the one and only…Gretchen.

The story was titled, 'The Door.'

When Gretchen and I broke up, I took all of her stuff that I had and mailed it off. The box included all of her court documents for her MIP charge, some clothes, and some other things.

The only thing I wanted back from Gretchen was my flat screen TV, which I had let her use in her room when she moved into her townhome. I had deleted her number, so I emailed her about it.

I asked, "May I please have my TV back?"

She responded and said, "Ok I will give it to Charlie (who was one of my good friends up there) and he can give it back to you."

That sounded fantastic! I didn't have to see her, and I get the TV back.

A few weeks went by, and I still hadn't heard anything. I emailed Gretchen again, and told her to please give the TV to Charlie so I can pick it up.

She responded, "I don't think I should have to give you back something that you gave to me as a gift."

I wrote back, "Oh, I'm sorry. Did the TV have a fucking bow wrapped around it when I gave it to you? I want it back now!"

She never replied.

As God as my witness, I was going to reclaim that $200 flat screen…even if it killed me.

My close friend John and I went back to our college town for a night of partying with some old fraternity brothers. Our fraternity was having a private party that night at a local bar, and we just wanted to feel like we were in college again. It was also the same town where the evil dweller Gretchen resided at the time.

Coincidence? Absolutely!

After John and a few friends of ours finished up at the bar, one of my buddies needed a ride home. Guess where he lived? Oh yes, the same neighborhood as Gretchen. It was fate.

John and I dropped off our friend at his place and as we were leaving we passed Gretchen's house of horrors.

I looked at John and said, "John. We go way back. Will you help me reclaim what is rightfully mine?"

John replied, "I think this is a very bad idea."

"It will be a quick in and out job."

Gretchen's car was not in the driveway, so I knew she wasn't home. She lived with two other girls and not one of them ever locked the front door.

I ran up to the door, and kicked it open as hard as I could. Gretchen's roommate Casey and her friend were watching a scary movie in the dark, so I essentially scared the living shit out of them.

Casey screamed, "OH MY GOD! PLEASE NOOOO!"

Like I was going to chop her head off or something.

Casey's friend jumped so high off the couch that her head hit the ceiling fan, which was operating at full speed. Her thick skull broke two of the fan blades in the process.

Once they both realized it was only me, Casey said, "What the hell are you doing here? Gretchen isn't here."

I yelled, "I know woman! Sit down and shut up!"

I went over to Gretchen's room, and opened the door. The flat screen was right inside, but I had forgotten that I had mounted it to the wall. I was going to need some tools to get it out of there. I looked at John and said, "Get your tool bag. This is going to take some work."

Casey finally realized what was happening.

She ran over to me and pleaded, "Please don't do this. You're just going to create a shit storm, and I don't want to deal with that."

I replied, "It's not my fault you live with a thieving slut!"

I then realized that taking the TV off the wall mount would be quite a task. When John came back inside with his tools I said, "There's been a change of plans."

Casey sighed in relief and said, "Thank God."

I asked, "John, you remember that time I had to buy a new door for Gretchen's room?"

He said, "Um, yeah."

"I'm taking that motherfucker back!"

John and I used his drill to unscrew the hinges to the door and disconnected it from her room. As we were both carrying the door out of the house, I looked at the girls and said, "Thank you for your cooperation. Have a good night!"

"Fuck you!" Casey screamed.

We threw the door in the back of his truck and drove all the way home.

Unfortunately, we didn't strap it down in any way. It managed to escape the bed of the truck, and when we got back home, it was gone.

I'm going to miss that door…now and forever.

The End.

After that story, the comedy show was complete. I was fortunate enough to get another standing ovation at the end, which was a huge surprise. The loud volume of cheering was music to my ears. I felt truly blessed to have all of those people with me that night. I was up on stage for an hour and twenty minutes, and it was one of the most amazing experiences of my life.

I made sure I went around the room after the show to thank each and every person for coming.

After that night, I felt that a big weight had been lifted off my shoulders. I was finally free from the depression that had been plaguing me for so long. All the negative feelings I had been holding in were finally exposed in a comedic fashion. I couldn't have been happier with the success of the 'Revenge' show.

I then realized that I shouldn't just sit around bitching about my past misfortunes. I should learn from my mistakes, and transform my tragic memories into something positive.

In turn, I will be stronger, and wiser than ever before.

My eyes were finally opened, and for the very first time, I saw a bright light shining into my world of darkness.

The Awakening

It was time now to start a new life. During the dark moments, I could not figure out exactly who I was. I was allowing these women take control of the gentlemen inside, and twisting him until he broke in half.

The mind as well as the body can only take so much abuse. My perception was being altered by the traumatic events I suffered through. Those events inadvertently made me more powerful than I could have possibly imagined. I have now become emotionally adaptable, and my heart has become self-aware. I will not let the evil actions of others warp my reality anymore. There is someone out there for me, but she has not been found yet.

Maybe I have been running into all the wrong women, but I believe that they were all placed into my life for a specific purpose. They were the elements that inevitably made me realize that my biggest fear was also my greatest strength.

Loneliness was the crutch that was preventing me from becoming who I wanted to be. I must be happy with myself, before anything else. I have also spent a lot of time learning about myself. I know now that I must be the man I have always been raised to be. I have a lot of work to do, but each day I am getting closer to becoming complete.

Performing at the comedy show helped me deal with the emotional pain extensively. I wanted to put myself out there, stripped down to the bone for everyone to see. I was able to harness my negative energy, and convert it into laughter. In doing so, I wiped away the dust from my troubled past. As I looked back at my life, and reminisced about the crazy relationships that once were, it now feels much better laughing, rather than crying.

I am nowhere close to being perfect, but I will try to forever be the best man I can to everyone who deserves the kindness of my heart.

No one should be treated like shit for trying to make someone happy.

If you feel like you're not having any luck with relationships, take a step back from it all. You must find yourself. Examine who you really are, and who you want to become.

Pursue the things that make you happy, and find your inner strength as I did.

How to Avoid Shitty Relationships:

1. If they cheat once they will do it again. Get rid of them.
2. Never change into something you don't want to be in order to love someone else.
3. If you can't trust the person you are with they are probably hiding something.
4. Stop doing the right things for the wrong people.
5. Don't let anyone take advantage of the kindness of your heart.
6. If alcohol affects the way your significant other treats you then they are too weak for a strong relationship with you.
7. If the person is fresh out of a break up chances are you are just a rebound. Proceed with caution.
8. Guard your heart until the time is right to open it up to someone else. Your love is very special and there are only certain individuals in this world who deserve it.
9. Never be afraid to tell the other person how you feel about something. Do not bottle up your feelings inside. Express them thoroughly.
10. Be yourself, no matter what.

How to Survive a Break-Up:

1. Out of sight, out of mind. Get rid of everything that was connected to the ex. Phone numbers, photos...EVERYTHING.
2. Do things you weren't able to do when you were with that person.
3. Start becoming more physically active and set goals for yourself.
4. Get in touch with friends and family that you may have neglected.
5. Find out what makes you happy and explore the hell out of it.
6. Get out of town and take a mini-vacation. Go somewhere you have never been before.
7. Start doing things spontaneously.
8. Find a hobby and run with it.
9. Avoid excessive alcohol consumption to suppress the pain.
10. When you're ready get yourself back in the dating game and don't be afraid of a one-night stand. As always, use protection.

Status Updates:

Jayden 'The Alcoholic Brainiac'

Update: She is now married to the same guy she started dating immediately after we broke up. She completed nursing school, and is now a Resident Nurse at a local hospital. She is also expecting her first child.

My Final Words: I hope that Jayden has a happy marriage and a healthy newborn child. I also hope that she will never have to visit a psychiatric hospital again as a patient.

Ravenna 'The Cocaine Tree Giant'

Update: She completed her degree in education and is now teaching at an elementary school. I believe she now has a steady boyfriend.

My Final Words: I hope that Ravenna discovers that cocaine is not the key to happiness. I pray for any child that may attend her classroom. To her newly found boyfriend…Godspeed brother.

Sydnie 'The Freshman Snake'

Update: She graduated college and moved back home. Once she was back home, she rekindled a relationship with her long time ex-boyfriend. She then subsequently cheated on him and is currently single.

My Final Words: I hope that Sydnie discovers that sluts never survive.

Gretchen 'The Psychotic Gremlin'

<u>Update:</u> She graduated with a degree in education. She has not found a job yet. She has become a serial cheater. She has cheated on every man she has been with after we broke up. She has also become a bit of an alcoholic, which has caused her excessive psychotic behavior to continue.

<u>My Final Words:</u> I hope that she one day comprehends the harmful effects of cheating. I also hope she gets medical help soon for her anger issues. I pray that I will never see the evil gremlin for as long as I live.

Carlisle 'The Virtual Girlfriend'

<u>Update:</u> She got back with her ex right after we broke up, and they have been on and off for about three years. She is still currently employed by the many lonely men of the world. No matter where I navigate online one of her ads always pops-up on my web browser.

<u>My Final Words:</u> I hope that Carlisle someday finds a more respectable career. I also hope she doesn't let her ex suck the money from her pocket like a fiend.

Aberdeen 'The Double Crossing Super Model'

<u>Update:</u> She is still currently active in the modeling world. She moved to another city to be closer to her parents. Her and her boyfriend eventually broke up and she is currently single.

<u>My Final Words</u>: I hope that Aberdeen will someday understand the value of a dollar and the harmful effects of lying. Some 'French kissing' classes wouldn't be such a bad idea either.

Chandler 'The Personal Trainer Sex Fiend'

<u>Update:</u> No status updates available. All connections to this woman have been terminated.

<u>My Final Words:</u> I hope that she gets medical help for her sex addiction and that she does not come into contact with any new venereal diseases.

Fawn 'The Wasted Witch'

<u>Update</u>: She spent eighteen days in the county jail for her DWI. She was unable to drive for a year and is now unemployed.

<u>My Final Words:</u> You may want to stop drinking…like forever.

<u>To All of the Women of My Past:</u> I forgive you for what you did to me. I do not wish any harm to befall you nor do I expect an apology. My only wish is for you to never do the things you did to me to anyone else.

Juddy 'The Nice Guy'

<u>Update:</u> I have become a much happier man. I no longer have hatred toward any of the women in my past. I have put my focus into activities that better myself and others around me. I have performed a total of five comedy shows. I plan on continuing to do stand-up comedy for as long as I can and helping others who are struggling as I once did. I am currently single.

<u>My Final Words:</u>

Dear Ex-Girlfriends,

    Thank you for transforming me into the man I am today. The things you did to me have made me more powerful than I could've possibly imagined. I hope that your life is filled with happiness and that one day you are able to meet someone to fall in love with.

    Sincerely,

    Mr. Nice Guy

The End

I Once Was a Nice Guy:

The hilarious and psychotic tales about the women of my past

Based on true stories

By: Juddy Ferguson

© 2014, Juddy Ferguson Self publishing

www.juddyferguson.com

Instagram: JuddyFerguson

FaceBook:www.facebook.com/juddyferguson

www.ingramcontent.com/pod-product-compliance
Lightning Source LLC
LaVergne TN
LVHW051514070426
835507LV00023B/3105